SOUL SEARCHER

THE TRUE STORY
OF A WOMAN'S
JOURNEY
TO FIND HEALING
AFTER THE TRAUMA
OF RAPE

JOANNE MUNTEAN

outskirts press

Soul Searcher
The True Story of a Woman's Journey to Find Healing after the Trauma of Rape
All Rights Reserved.
Copyright © 2019 Joanne Muntean
v3.0

The opinions expressed in this manuscript are solely the opinions of the author and do not represent the opinions or thoughts of the publisher. The author has represented and warranted full ownership and/or legal right to publish all the materials in this book.

This book may not be reproduced, transmitted, or stored in whole or in part by any means, including graphic, electronic, or mechanical without the express written consent of the publisher except in the case of brief quotations embodied in critical articles and reviews.

Outskirts Press, Inc.
http://www.outskirtspress.com

Paperback ISBN: 978-1-9772-0125-6

Cover Photo © 2019 www.gettyimages.com. All rights reserved - used with permission.

Outskirts Press and the "OP" logo are trademarks belonging to Outskirts Press, Inc.

PRINTED IN THE UNITED STATES OF AMERICA

Table of Contents

INTRODUCTION — i
PROLOGUE — v

THE EARLY YEARS

CHAPTER 1 — 1
CHAPTER 2 — 5
CHAPTER 3 — 7
CHAPTER 4 — 10
CHAPTER 5 — 12
CHAPTER 6 — 14
CHAPTER 7 — 16
CHAPTER 8 — 18

THE MIDDLE YEARS BEFORE

CHAPTER 9 — 26
CHAPTER 10 — 32
CHAPTER 11 — 35

THE EVENT

CHAPTER 12 — 40

THE AFTERMATH

CHAPTER 13 — 50

THE MIDDLE YEARS AFTER

CHAPTER 14	54
CHAPTER 15	58
CHAPTER 16	63
CHAPTER 17	67
CHAPTER 18	71

THE LATER YEARS

CHAPTER 19	76
CHAPTER 20	79
CHAPTER 21	82
CHAPTER 22	85
EPILOGUE	94
ACKNOWLEDGMENTS	98

INTRODUCTION

This is my story and the time has come to tell it. Parts of it were written long ago. Other parts just a few years ago. And still other parts were totally unknown to me until very recently.

It hasn't been an easy story to put together. It does have a beginning, a middle, and an end. But the middle was written before the beginning, and I had to wait until I was in my 70's to see how it might end. Even now at 73, I feel as if I'm still living the end of the story. I always will be as long as I'm still around.

This is not a memoir. This is not a book about my children, my husbands, my work, not even about me exactly. For there would certainly be many more things I would tell if it were simply a story of my life. However, it definitely is about something that *happened* to me, and how it affected my life from that point on. It is about the times in which I grew up and how, as children, we can each be so influenced by those around us. God knows there are many people with more interesting and entertaining stories to tell. There are thousands who have lived through my experience. I didn't go on any great adventures. I didn't discover anything that would better mankind. I never made a lot of money. I'm just an average, ordinary person who grew up believing life would work out well for me.

So just what is it that I found so important about my average, ordinary life that I felt moved to write a book about it?

To be honest, until very recently, I didn't think this would happen. That now makes perfect sense to me. Because why tell a story when you don't know how it ends. Why even start a story if it seems to have no purpose? That's where I was in my life until about two years ago. It was at that time things started coming together and the nonsense began to make sense. It's taken me those couple of years to live in this new space, experience life in this more colorful, more nuanced place, and breathe in this cleaner, clearer air before I was ready to talk about what happened.

I feel now I am ready to share with others the events and experiences of my life that ended up taking me on this journey that lasted too long and stole from me the very essence of who I really am.

I tell this story for two reasons. One, it finishes the journey for me. Putting my account into the public realm is the way I have chosen to be brave enough to not hide any of what I once thought of as shaming, limiting and diminishing occurrences in my life. Second, I would hope by telling what happened to me and its life-altering affect, it might save even one other person years of wondering why and how their life is unfolding the way it is. It may look like it's working from the outside, but inside is soul-stealing sadness, darkness, and depression. Few of us can risk a direct peek inside, so it becomes a lot like feeling you don't belong. A lot like feeling there's something missing. A lot like feeling you just don't fit into your skin any longer. Those were the feelings I was experiencing. I always told myself that my life was unfolding just as it was meant to. That all those hopes and desires I had as a child and adolescent didn't amount to anything but daydreams and wishful thinking. And when my life started opening like an effortlessly blossoming rose, I simply accepted its promise and ignored the browning edges on the petals and the sagging stem.

I believe I knew, on some level at least, that I was meant for far more than what I settled for. Yet, I followed the path I'd begun and just kept going. I never kept a diary, but I did write lots of poetry throughout my late teens, twenties and early thirties. All of which I saved. So, it was amazing for me to go back and read my poetry so many years later and see the various periods of my life laid out so clearly in those writings. Those poems I wrote turned out to provide the key that would unlock a mystery that haunted me most of my adult life.

I felt certain that at some point in my life I had finally begun to mature emotionally. I felt confident that I had begun to grow up. I was so proud of myself for bravely taking the steps I needed to take to be mother to my children, landlord at my duplex, and office manager at a full-time job. Although those were difficult and, in many ways, very trying years, for the most part I was happy and excited about this new path I found myself on and this more grownup way I found myself to be. In spite of the new challenges I faced each day, I felt fuller and brighter, more satisfied and content than I ever had before. Life for me had finally begun. That rose was looking pretty perky and the stem was growing stronger and straighter every day!

Then something happened. I didn't know at the time how this event would affect me for the rest of my days. But now, in retrospect, I see so clearly that it has. This is what this story is about. This is why I want to tell you my tale.

Burying bad things that happen to us don't make them go away. Just stuffing it deep inside doesn't heal the wounds. Especially if we don't even know the wounds are there. If trauma isn't faced and dealt with openly, loudly, angrily, and tearfully, it will quietly and secretly run your entire life. This then is my story.

PROLOGUE

I HAD PTSD before PTSD had a name! There were no cell phones or internet. No fast or easy way to call for help. I was on my own. As I lay curled in a ball between my bed and the cold wall behind me, I felt my heart beating like a bass drum in my chest. I waited for a sound, a footfall, maybe the crash of a door, that would let me know I was no longer safe. I already knew my children and I were no longer alone in my house.

This must be what it felt like for a soldier in a foxhole just waiting to be overrun by the enemy. Waiting to be discovered. Waiting to feel a bullet rip into their body. Waiting to be killed. I held the phone in my hand while it rang and rang the number I had dialed.

Five minutes before this, I had been lying in bed. Not asleep. Watching shadows move across the ceiling and walls of my bedroom. I was tired, but every time I closed my eyes I saw that figure standing in the doorway of my bedroom. It looked like a dark shadow backlit by the light in the hallway, a dark and foreboding silhouette.

My eyes would fly open to see an empty doorway. No form, no shape, no body standing there. It was my imagination. But it was also so real that I couldn't allow my eyes to close. I could never stop watching, being vigilant for that shape that had so invaded the safety and security of my being.

Although I tried to sleep, to give my exhausted body a rest, there was now that part of me that needed to stay alert and vigilant so that this time I might be ready if the terror came again. And I'm sure it was this part of me that heard the jiggling of the doorknob on the basement door as someone tried to turn the knob and open the door. The door that was just down the hall from where I lay in my bed.

I sat up. Did I hear what I thought I heard? I silently crept out of bed and to the doorway of my room. My children's bedrooms were one across the hall from mine and the other just next to mine. Their doors were slightly open, and all was quiet inside. I started tiptoeing down the hallway toward that door where I heard the noise, when suddenly a light came on behind that door. The light spilled out from under the door onto the carpet in the hallway. Now I knew there was someone behind that door. I knew who it was. And I knew what he wanted.

That's when the fear hit me. Right in the gut like a sack full of rocks. As quickly and quietly as I could, I got back to my room. I grabbed the phone by my bed and laid down to hide, phone in hand. As I waited for the sheriff's department to answer my call, I cringed with fear, my insides screaming "Not again! Please, God, not again!"

THE EARLY YEARS

CHAPTER 1

I AM A child of the 1950's. Came of age during the 1960's. It was the time of Vietnam, flower children, rock and roll, open sex and a very relaxed drug culture. Of course, I missed many of those changes as I was married in 1964 and was busy working, mothering and homemaking. I was never quite a "baby boomer." I was much more a product of the generation of my parents. Even though I didn't always feel comfortable, the pull to listen and obey was strong enough to hold me there. My life was unfolding very unremarkably, just as my parents, my church, my teachers and our culture said it should.

I was raised in one of those post WWII two-bedroom, one-bath, bungalow-style houses with the attached one-car garage. There were hundreds of these homes built in our area in the mid 1940's as soldiers and their families came home to begin living life after years of facing death.

Dad had the upstairs finished with paint, plaster, and hardwood floors so that his two daughters could someday share that space. I was three years old. My sister was newborn. Dad also had the open porch enclosed between the house and that barely-big-enough garage. That gave him a space to read his newspaper and listen to baseball games without being underfoot in my mother's house.

I believe we grew up in our middle-class 50's neighborhood as most others of that era. We lived on a cul-de-sac, which back then we all called a circle street. There were twelve houses on our little street. Eight of which all looked like ours with the four at the top of the circle slightly different, slightly larger. We gathered at the neighbors to watch The Texaco Star Theatre with Milton Berle because they were the first ones on our street to get a television set.

I got good grades — all A's grades one through eight. I was picked to be an eighth-grade cheerleader, not because of any athletic ability, but because I got good grades and the teachers liked me. I couldn't even skip! In high school I made National Honor Society and graduated ninth in my class of almost 300 students. Of course, I didn't go on to college. I didn't want to be a teacher, and I already had a boyfriend. My life was unfolding just as unremarkably as everyone thought it should.

I tried to follow the rules. I tried to be a good girl. Tried to do everything that was expected of me. Tried to be nice, polite and kind. Of course, I didn't always succeed. There was always that ornery, irascible, kid part of me that couldn't stay hidden. She would pop out, do her thing, accept the consequences, and then quietly disappear. As I got older, I reined her in and kept her quiet. But as a child, she was, at times, a joy to experience.

∽

"Joanne Rae Muntean" get into this house immediately!" She yelled as she banged the breezeway door to our tree-filled backyard.

"Oh, Lord," I sighed. "I'm in trouble again." You always knew if your full name was called, nothing good could follow. May as well give up my game of salt & pepper with my neighborhood friends and see what terrible crime I would be charged with and exactly what my penance would be.

Head drooping, shoulders sagging, and fear pumping through my veins, I reluctantly followed my mother's imposing backside into our little house to see what horrible act I would be accused of. As I shuffled into the house, I tried to recall what misdeeds I had recently been guilty of – both those known and unknown to my mother. At least to my eight-year-old mind, I didn't think she could possibly be aware of every infraction of which I had been guilty. But what if I was wrong? I thought my mother might have had super natural powers to be able to ferret out and identify any mischief of which I might have been a part.

Having become a mother myself, I know that wasn't true. But to a small, frightened little girl, the thought itself was enough.

"You stole money, young lady!" mother announced with eyes flashing fire and a face fixed in anger.

"No, I did not steal!" I answered, totally shocked at such an absurd accusation. I have been guilty of many things in my short, unremarkable life, but never stealing! The one thought that sailed through my mind in that fractious moment was the only larceny I had ever committed was when I would sneak into my bedroom and take money from my own allowance to spend on penny candy at the neighborhood market. But I knew I never had – nor ever would – steal from someone else! I didn't want to go to Hell! And everything I had learned from my parents and my church preached that was one quick way to get there. That, and not following the rules, of course.

So it was with total belief and conviction in my own innocence I stood up as tall and strong as my eight-year-old self could muster. I looked up at my mother and said "No! I did not steal!"

So sure was I in my own blamelessness that her next words washed over me with such startling surprise that my skinny little legs almost let me down.

"It had to be you!" she rebuffed through gritted teeth, "You were the only one in the house when I left. I put six one-dollar bills on the table by the front door to pay the man who fixed my sweeper. Now there are only five! It had to be you who took it!" The color in her cheeks rose as the timber of her voice soared to a shrill and accusatory apex. She sneered down at me with anger and fury etched into the lines of her normally beautiful face, awaiting my reply.

In one blinding, heart-stabbing moment, I knew I was doomed. I didn't steal that one dollar bill. But in order to prove my innocence, I would have to admit to committing another mortal sin, that of not following the rules. For I had not been the only person in our house when mother left to run her errand.

CHAPTER 2

ONE OF THE major rules enforced in our house was that we were to have no friends over when parents weren't home. This was not simply a rule but a regulation set in stone which, if not adhered to, could be followed by capital punishment. Or so it seemed to me as that conflicted child of eight.

I did not steal that dollar bill. But I did allow one of my classmates into my house when neither of my parents was home. Therein lay the conundrum of my situation.

I wish I could have been honest with my mother and explained to her how this homely little boy from my third-grade class, more stranger than friend, had been invited by me, admittedly, into my home during a time I knew he shouldn't have been there. That conversation, unfortunately for all, was not to be.

It didn't matter that he was bullied by the other kids, made fun of, and treated as an outcast, never included or accepted by the other children. I felt sorry for him. I brought him home, just like I did other wounded, damaged and distressed living things I found on my childhood playground.

That in no way excused the action I took which resulted in that missing dollar bill. The rule was valid and sound, sensible and wise.

And there needed to be a consequence to me for having broken it.

Yet it broke my heart that I couldn't share my feelings with my mother. I knew I had done wrong, and I fully expected to pay a price for the choice I made. But my feelings were important, too, and I deserved to be listened to – even if it changed nothing.

I finally admitted to letting my classmate into the house while my mother was gone. I guess I perceived that to be the lesser of the two sins. But I wanted her to understand why I made the decision I made, even if I remained guilty as charged. By denying even a hearing of my emotions and beliefs, I learned, as I always did, how unimportant those things were. How what was always of greatest importance, what always mattered most, was whether the rules were followed and whether the will of authority was adhered to.

To this day, I don't know where that one dollar bill went. Maybe my little classmate took it or maybe he didn't. I do know that I was made to pay back that money – as well I should have been. Of course, for my eight-year-old child, this seemed a nearly insurmountable task as I only earned ten cents per week for my allowance. But more consequential was the injury to my psychological well-being because it sent the message to me that if allowed to make choices on my own, I would fail miserably. I could not take care of myself. I would always need an authority figure to choose for me.

I'm sure this was not the lessen my parents set out to teach me. It was, however, the lessen I learned. And learn it well, I did.

CHAPTER 3

DONE WELL, CREATING rules and the atmosphere in which they are to be obeyed can create a feeling of safety and security for those encompassed in their structure. We all need rules to survive. How could we drive our cars if there were no traffic laws? How could we be part of a thriving, safe and fair society if there are no rules by which individuals and groups are governed?

Individual families need rules too. I don't dispute that fact. And they are needed for the same reasons societies at large need rules – for control of the safety and well-being of each person involved. However, when rules are made within families, these rules need to be discussed by all members affected regardless of age or gender. Although the discussion should be open and equal, I do NOT believe that votes should be. Parents, or caregivers of younger members, need a more weighted say in whatever regulations will be set down to operate within the family structure. Hopefully, for at least moderately functional families, these rules will be fair, impartial and obeyed, even if disagreed upon by the more minor members of the family

A broken rule should never mean a broken bone or a broken spirit. Those entrusted with the management of rules need to be as fair and just as the rules themselves. Domination by fear simply breeds more fear and will eventually lead to some form of revolt.

I'm sure that that one incident of the missing one dollar bill did not push me over the precipice into an abyss of self-doubt and hesitancy. I know there were many other young-child attempts at making my way in the world and stepping bravely out on my own. Most did not end well. Several I remember quite vividly.

There was the time I decided, at about age five, that I would walk alone to my cousin's house. He was my very favorite cousin, and I was sure he would grow up to be my husband. He lived about three blocks from my home. I didn't ask if I could go for I knew permission would never be granted. So I just went.

My cousin was three years older than I. Yet it never occurred to me that he would be in school that day. So off I went on my own to have an adventure that belonged only to me. In order to get to his house, I had to cross two streets – not busy but, nonetheless, streets. It seemed such a long walk for my short toddler legs until finally I recognized the little red brick bungalow with the attached screened-in porch so like my very own house but yet so much bigger and better because it was made of bricks! I entered into the enclosed breezeway and knocked on the back door. I rapped gently at first and then with more determination. Finally, from inside I heard a voice asking who was there.

"It's me, Jo, your cousin" I yelled back, recognizing my cousin's voice.

"Come in. The door's unlocked." He answered back. Another nod to the times in which we lived. "I'm upstairs in my bedroom."

So in I went. I did, indeed, find him upstairs, which was where I thought all children's bedrooms were located. He was in bed and immediately suggested I not get too close as he had the flu or a bad cold or some other germy thing. In fact, his mother, my aunt, was at that very moment at the drug store getting him something to relieve his cough and sniffles.

Had he not been sick that day, he would have been in school and my visit would have been a failure. As it was, I was quite proud of myself having ventured three blocks, crossing two streets, and actually finding this very home. Great work for a five-year-old!

My stay lasted only about ten minutes and it was decided by both of us that I should head back home. Halfway home my great adventure ended in disgrace. For one block and one street-crossing from home, I met my mother.

One of my little friends, who declined to make the journey with me, had ratted me out. I don't believe I had ever seen my mother as angry as she was that day. As an adult, I totally understand her ire. She was probably reacting more out of fear for my safety than anything else. But I still would like to believe that I would have handled it differently.

All I remember from the rest of that little jaunt for me was the spanking I got the remaining way home. Each foot fall landed with a hand slap to my backside. I know I cried loudly with each swat, probably as much out of fear and embarrassment as pain. I never went to see my cousin alone again. Not even when I was old enough to cross streets and to walk myself to school and back.

That was only one of the ways I learned very early that adventure could get you in lots of trouble and terrible things could happen if you poked your nose (or your finger) where it didn't belong.

CHAPTER 4

BACK WHEN MY family first moved into our new home, there were still other houses being finished on our cul-de-sac of young families and lots of kids. Of course, as a child, it was a natural curiosity to want to see each of these houses in their varied stages of completion.

I'll never forget one particular weekend when I decided to take a closer look around one of the houses being finished at the top of our circle street. I poked around the open porch area between the house and garage. I climbed over lumber and building materials, checking out all the wires and brackets, bolts and boards that were contained in that small space. I saw one particularly interesting opening that I could just touch if I reached up as far as I could. Of course, that was a challenge I just couldn't resist. So I stood on tippy toes and poked my finger right into that hole. Turned out it was some kind of electrical outlet which hadn't been finished, and I felt a shock from the tip of that finger all the way down my arm. As a young child, I really didn't know what had happened. I just knew I had done something I wasn't supposed to do – and it hurt! I grabbed my hand and ran home.

I guess I was looking not only for confirmation that I was not going to die, but also sympathy for the discomfort I had caused myself. What I actually got, at least in my memory, was a pretty quick dismissal by a dad who really didn't want to put down his newspaper. To his credit, his first questions were to make sure I was OK. After that, there was simply an admonishment to stop poking around new construction areas.

I had acted stupidly again. I had done something for which I knew I could get in trouble. I had again made a decision, on my own, and gotten hurt.

So along with learning that it's not a good idea to stick your finger into a hole you know nothing about, I also learned that not following the rules and making my own decisions led to a painful outcome for me.

I wanted to do better. I wanted to follow the rules. I wanted to be a good girl. It was just difficult. It seemed like every time I courageously stepped out on my own to bravely test the waters of my own life, something went wrong. My attempts at individuality and independence usually ended badly for me. But I remember another part of me, too.

I loved to be in charge of the younger children in the neighborhood. During the summer, I led craft days in our backyard for the little kids. We played "restaurant" with the penny candy we bought from the market. We used our bicycles and wagons to make carnival rides. We decorated pillow cases, called ourselves The Vamps and ran around the neighborhood. Only in backyards, of course. We weren't allowed to run on the front grass of most of those little homes. I wrote and directed plays that my playmates would perform for our parents. Obviously, there was a bit of the boss in me. I wish she had hung in there a little longer and been a little tougher.

There has always been a part of me, even in childhood, that found peace and calm in contemplating the world and people around me. I knew those quiet parts of myself were real, too. I'm sure the adults around me saw it all as daydreaming. But that quest into my own thoughts and feelings was a very important part of who I was — and who I am.

CHAPTER 5

I KNOW I was always a sensitive and very introspective child. I liked nothing more than to sit in silence, taking in with all my senses my natural surroundings.

I found a quiet space at the side of my garage where I could lay in the grass and watch the summer clouds change shapes as they moved across the sky. I made up stories about the monsters and dragons I saw moving and melting into witches and goblins. I saw animals with opened mouths and leaping bodies chasing running children then watching as they all disappeared into wispy mist. As I got older, I liked to look for people in the shapes and shadows of the clouds that danced overhead. Sometimes I'd be quite successful. Yet, as all clouds do, too quickly the shapes would change, dissolve, and melt away.

I loved to sit at the western window of the bedroom I shared with my sister. Since our bedroom was the upstairs of that bungalow-style home, the walls were short and the ceiling slanted so that I could sit on the floor and look out the window which looked out onto the top of our circle street. Close to the beginning of the arc of the road stood a streetlight. Many nights, unknown to everyone – even my sister, I think – I sat and watched the rain or the snow swirl around the light cast by the glow of that streetlamp. It was a wonderful place from which to contemplate my world. It was one of my favorite places to be as a child. I found it very peaceful and calming.

Another place that brought me joy was sitting all alone on the peaked roof of the finished breezeway between my house and garage. I found that by raising the window at the eastern end of my upstairs bedroom and taking out the screen, I could carefully navigate through that open space right onto the porch roof.

It was an incredibly advantageous spot from which to view the cotton candy layers of light and color as the sun rose just for me. It also proved to be the best place ever to see the carpet of twinkling stars above my little-girl body and try so very hard to find the different constellations and name the brightest stars. I watched all the different phases of the moon as it waxed and waned just for my pleasure. These clear, cloudless nights became my planetarium.

Of course, that would many times lead me down the path of trying to imagine what it would be like when there were no stars, no sun, no moon, no house, no sister, no mom, no dad, no———. Well, not even a word "no". What was nothing? And how could it even be grasped if there was nothing left by which to describe it. That's usually where it ended for me. My child brain could go no further, and it probably took me right back to that place of fear, where I seemed to be living so much of my childhood.

CHAPTER 6

MANY TIMES AS an adult, I've tried to figure out just where all this fear had come from. I do know that as a sensitive child I took to heart much of what I was taught by teachers, parents, church and society. I grew up in a time when it was acceptable teaching that girls were the weaker sex. It was okay if girls were needy and had to be taken care of. We were even told to allow the boys to win at games so it wouldn't harm their egos. We were never taught to be strong, to have a clear and powerful voice, to be fighters and winners. Never counselled to dream big and take action to make those dreams come true.

It was a time when children were seen and not heard. A time when girls went to college to become teachers. Or could further their education, if college wasn't right, by studying to become a nurse. If neither of those career paths were chosen, you could be a secretary. I told my father the summer before my junior year in high school that I wanted to go to work in one of the dress shops in our local mall. My career idea was to get a job in sales and work my way up to be a buyer and go to New York or some other fantastical place. My father told me that I would be a secretary. With two years of shorthand and two years of typing, the day after graduation I began working — as a secretary.

So even as a child, the deck was stacked against me. I really did try hard to be that good girl that I knew everyone wanted to see, but I also knew that I was never the perfect child. For deep down I had lots of thoughts about how I saw life and how I thought it should be so different. And when I couldn't hold back these feelings of anger and uncertainty, they would be met with disdain and disbelief by those around me. I heard many times while growing up, "I don't like this girl. I like the nice one." Of course, I took that message to mean (as I'm sure it did!) that I was to listen to my elders, remain agreeable and smiling, and never display anger or frustration. And just before a slap across the face "Don't look at me like that!" I remember actually running into our bathroom and looking into the mirror to see what I might have looked like so I wouldn't do it again. Getting slapped hurt! I believe now that probably whenever a look of anger or annoyance flashed across my face, even if I was unaware of it, mother saw it, reacted without thought, and slapped me. This was just one more way that I learned my feelings didn't matter. Pushing down the anger and always trying to please was the way I learned to survive in my family and in the world.

My dad and I used to have this little game we played. He would say to me "I don't LIKE you." To which I was to frown and look unhappy. Then he would follow with "I LOVE you." At which time my part was to smile and look happy. But I never was really happy for I wanted to be liked, too. I knew that all parents were supposed to "love" their children. But I wanted more than that. I wanted to be known and LIKED for who I was.

Home is supposed to be your soft place to fall. The place where you are loved unconditionally. The place where you can feel safe to be who you really are. I don't know how many of us actually got to experience that. I know I didn't, and I fear I've passed that legacy onto my own children. Maybe they'll be smarter than I and break that chain of unfortunate behavior. Maybe not.

CHAPTER 7

I SAW MYSELF as stupid, unattractive, unpopular and poor. Most of this really negative self-judgment came with becoming a teenager. I just always felt I never fit in.

All through grade school mom had a rule (RULES again!) that her children would only wear two outfits per week to school. Being a good rule follower, usually, I would wear one outfit Monday and Tuesday, a different outfit Wednesday and Thursday, and whichever one was cleanest, would be worn on Friday. Of course, we always came home from school and changed into "play clothes" so our "school clothes" would stay clean. And since mom did the laundry each week, she knew if that rule was being followed.

I will never forget early in my freshman year in high school sitting in home room and noticing a girl I didn't even know who kept staring at me. After several days of this, I could stand it no longer and finally asked her what she was staring at.

"You wore the same clothes yesterday that you have on today." She calmly replied.

"Yeah," I answered back "they're not dirty!" This, for me, would have been the only reason to wear something different.

It was after that exchange that I began looking at the other high school girls. They each wore something different to school every day! I was mortified. Why had I never noticed how the other girls dressed? Because you just didn't question mother's rules! After that embarrassing encounter with a fellow student, I made sure never again to wear the same clothes two days in a row to school. But for me, the damage was done. Once again, I was senseless, humiliated and embarrassed. Somehow I should have known this was how it was done. All the other kids knew it. At least to my young, easily persuaded mind, they all got it, except for me.

That same year I remember being invited to a boy/girl party at a friend's house. Of course, I knew it would be a "make-out" party. Never having been allowed to date before high school, I really wanted to go. The only problem was, I had never been to a party like that and had no idea what to do or how to do it. So, I confided in two girls I thought were my friends, telling them that I had never kissed a boy before and didn't know how.

They patiently explained to me how to practice by kissing the back of my own hand and assured me I would do just fine. I had no idea how stupid they must have thought I was because when I went to school the next day, I found they had blabbed to all our friends what I had told them. Everyone had a good laugh at my expense. And, once again, I got to feel shamed and embarrassed. How could I get such good grades and still be so damn dumb! For all the smarts I possessed, I really felt so utterly incapable. It only added to my belief that, on my own, all I would create would be trouble and bad judgement. Surely, what I had learned was true — I needed someone to take care of me.

CHAPTER 8

ALONG WITH CAREGIVER persons in our lives, so important as we grow up, we also have that protective "mother" instinct within. As we mature and grow, we learn to lean on and trust that inner intuitive nature to know what is best for us. These intuitive feelings grow stronger as our physical caregivers are letting out the rope and allowing us more freedom to make decisions on our own. This is the way we test the waters and learn to develop through experience and trial and error our own conscious truths about danger, love, responsibility and being.

During this time when our own instincts begin to develop, we so need to be able to share these inner urgings with others who may understand and know so much more than we do about life experiences and the difficulties we may be facing. It is a time when these feelings need nurturing and support so that we learn to honor those inner impulses and allow them to grow stronger within us. Unfortunately, this is not something much valued in our society. And it certainly is a time, usually during those teenage years, when we actually believe our parents know nothing. Real conversation never takes place, and we may be testing those waters with others who know as little as we do about life's truth.

What I needed to let go of within me for this maturation process to begin was that loving, caring, ever-present and always-in-charge, too-good mother part of my brain. She took such good care of me when I was very young. But I needed now to trust a different part of myself. This was an exceptionally difficult task for me because my actual beloved mother was a bit of a perfectionist, and I learned so well from her. She cared more about what others would say than what she or her own children were thinking and feeling. I don't fault her, as I'm sure this was exactly how she too was raised.

But I really needed her to back off a bit, give me some space, talk WITH me, not AT me, and allow me to make mistakes. I believed that making a mistake would probably end the world. I knew how important it was to my mom what other people thought and said about all of us. I never wanted to appear stupid, or uninformed, or silly, or lazy, or ugly, or unpleasant. I loved my mother with all my heart and wanted to please her. So too many times I went along with what she wanted even if I felt I had a really good argument against it. I wanted to have that discussion with her but was too afraid to begin it. So I just went along with most of what my mother told me. Because of this, I never had the freedom from my mother, nor my inner psychic mother either, to grow and explore. I didn't have the courage to examine the values and attitudes I was taught early in my life to see if these long-held beliefs were still true and worthy of being sustained. I especially needed to examine those beliefs which made my life too safe, which overprotected me, and made me fearful.

Even after I graduated from school, got a job, got married and had children, I still kept this inner too-good mother with me and in charge way past her time of usefulness. My own mother had let go, allowing me my own life, although she was quick to point out any errors she might perceive. All that I had learned as a child, could never let go of, and now allowed to run my life drove me into such well-worn ruts I felt I might never be able to escape.

Because I let this happen to me, I never learned to value the very things that made me uniquely me. What a waste of time were my inner urgings, my art, my music, my writing, my soul searching. I had learned all there was to know about being a good girl, sweet thing, smiley face, and niceness ninny. I learned well. I was respectful, kind, considerate, empathetic, sympathetic, reasonable, helpful and humble. I would surely go to heaven. The problem for me was I acted out all those traits with everyone except myself. To have been those things with myself would have been selfish and prideful. So it was easy for me see all others as children of God. I, however, was an orphan. Never quite good enough, no matter how hard I tried to fit in.

I share this because it so set me up for what happened later in my life. In trying to understand how I got from "here" to "there" it was necessary to travel many years back into my childhood. For there the seeds of "who we will become" are sown.

I also share with you a poem I wrote years into adulthood. I believe it was a cry from deep within me that needed to be heard.

Once upon a time…
There was a beautiful little girl.
She lived in the house next door.
She ran.
She played.
She laughed
She dreamed.
She dreamed of becoming a great actress when she grew up.

One day
She told her mother what she dreamed.
"Hmmmm," said her mother,
"I think you SHOULD be
a nurse or a teacher."
She told her father what she dreamed.
"You SHOULDN'T be so vain."
said her father,
not looking up from his newspaper.

So the little girl
dreamed some more.
She dreamed of becoming a doctor
and healing all the sick children
In the world.
But when she shared her dream
with her teacher,
she was told:
"You SHOULDN'T spend
So much time day dreaming.
You SHOULD use that time
to do your homework."

But it was difficult

CHAPTER 8

to stop dreaming...
So the little girl didn't.
She dreamed
of becoming a great lawyer
who would advocate
the rights of all children.
But her grandmother said
that would take
too many years of school
and too much money.
Maybe she SHOULD
just get married and
have children of her own.

The older the little girl got,
the more advice she got –
And the less she dreamed.

You SHOULD earn lots of money.
You SHOULDN'T waste your time dreaming.
You SHOULD do what girls do.
You SHOULDN'T ask so many questions.
You SHOULD be a good girl.
You SHOULD get good grades.
You SHOULD behave yourself.
You SHOULD do as you are told.

And so the little girl grew up
listening to them all –
All the SHOULDs and SHOULDN'Ts.

And guess what the little girl was when
she grew up...

UNHAPPY!

THE MIDDLE YEARS BEFORE

CHAPTER 9

I WAS A young woman now. Would soon become a wife, a mother. I would have three children. I would start college and make career changes. And I would enter into three marriages and survive three divorces. The last two were certainly not my vision for a future while daydreaming as an impressionable teenager.

I kept looking for someone to fill me up and complete me. Yet, I still wanted to hold the reins and be the boss. It felt like there was something, someone, inside me always trying to break through the walls I'd put up. Trying to get free. Wanting to grow up. But I beat her down. I shut her up. I let her know she'd only screw things up if I let her be in charge. So she stopped fighting. She disappeared into the rabbit hole again, into that deep, dark place I kept her hidden in for too many years.

As the years went by, those values, beliefs and behaviors, both conscious and unconscious, taught to me as a child grew stronger and stronger within me. Love everyone. Be kind to everyone. Don't show your anger. Put your own needs last. Do as you are told. Everyone else is more important than you are. Your feelings don't matter. So I gathered up all those lessons in my psyche and kept them ever present and closely protected. My parents had let go of me, but I continued to play, over and over again in my mind, all the things I had learned from them when I was a child. I imbued those teachings with more power than they deserved and slapped myself psychically every time I didn't live up to one of their edicts.

It wasn't surprising that I found a boyfriend at age sixteen. I needed someone to make me feel safe and protected. I had done my best to emotionally separate from my parents but still wanted that authority figure in my life. I chose someone two years older than I was, already graduated from high school, gainfully employed and the proud owner of a functioning car. That checked off all the boxes for me at the unsophisticated age of sixteen. He also had a very authoritarian personality which suited my needs perfectly. Besides, my best girlfriend had found a boyfriend so what was I to do. I felt I would either be left out, or included as one extra, with them. Neither idea appealed to me. So I simply found my own boyfriend. Now my friend and I could do things together. We could be four, not three.

Since I was sixteen and he was eighteen when we started dating, suffice it to say we didn't just hold hands for the three years before we married. There was some pretty heavy petting going on in those make-out sessions we had. Teenagers were no different back when I was young as they are today. But because I was such a good little church girl, I always felt like "damaged goods." The only way I could deal with all the guilt I felt was to tell myself it was okay because we would get married. He would still be the only man who had ever "touched" me. We both agreed that we would never "go all the way" until we were married. I certainly learned there were lots of other things two teenagers in lust could do that didn't involve actual sexual intercourse. But the guilt I heaped on myself stood in the way of me making any kind of really informed decision about my future. I remember my mother saying to me a few months before we got married "I know you better than you know yourself, and he is not the right one for you." I know now that my mother was absolutely right. But at age nineteen, I thought I knew everything so I didn't listen. Besides, I had all that guilt to deal with!

CHAPTER 9

We were still together when I graduated from high school at eighteen. He was twenty, and his dad had just retired from his job. His parents planned to sell their house and most of their belongings and move to Florida where they could enjoy nice weather all year round. I remember his mother saying to me before they left that she never could have left her son had she not known I was there to take care of him. Wow! As an extremely immature eighteen year old, that statement made my blood run cold. If I could have been honest, could have been truthful with his mother, I would have told her I was incapable of taking care of myself, let alone her twenty-year-old son. But, of course for many reasons, I felt the die had been cast. There was no way I could graciously extricate myself from this relationship nor stop the trajectory of its finish. So I married this young man, whom I shall refer to as man1, one cold and rainy day in February, 1964. I wasn't even twenty years old!

We had moved up our wedding date as all this took place during those turbulent years of the Vietnam War. In those years all teenage boys, when turning eighteen, became eligible for a draft into the armed services by the government of the United States. Eventually, this law forced a change in another law. Legal voting age at that time was twenty-one. The argument was made, and ultimately accepted, that if a young person was old enough at the age of eighteen to be drafted into fighting for his country, then that person should be allowed to vote. The law was changed. Our wedding date was moved forward because single men, not in college, were being drafted. However, married men were not.

So it was on that ugly, rainy day in February, I married man1. I remember walking down the aisle thinking "Stop! Stop! This isn't what I want to do!" But on the outside, I just smiled and acted as if all was well. That's how a good girl behaves. I was just doing what many young girls my age at that time were doing. And it was what everyone presumed would happen. We had been together for three years. So regardless of the inner warnings I may have had, I did what was expected of me.

We were both working at the same company from which his father had retired. He decided, and of course I agreed, we would live on my income and save his. This didn't leave much money for any extras. I worked 8-5 and he worked an afternoon shift 2-10:30. I would rush home from work every day on my lunch hour so we could eat lunch together — a lunch I had prepared before going to work that morning. Then before I left to go back to work, I would pack his lunchbox so he could take it to work with him. Then I would have to rush back to my job and ring that time card in before my hour was up.

When I got home from work in the evening, the first thing I did was clean up the table, sink, counter and stove from the remnants of our earlier lunch together. Never would I have dreamed of asking him to even put our dirty dishes in the sink. And neither would he have thought to do it for me! Of course, we didn't have a dishwasher — just me! I'd be ready for bed by 10:00 PM, but since man1 didn't get home from work until almost 11:00 PM, and he was never ready to go to sleep when he got home, I would end up keeping him company until he finally was ready to crash. That was usually around midnight. I was exhausted.

Friday nights were special. After cleaning up the kitchen, I would clean the entire two-bedroom, one-bath apartment from top to bottom. It wasn't big, but it took me most of the evening. Then I would wash and towel-dry our car so it would be clean when I picked up my husband from work when his shift ended at 10:30 PM. Then, if he saw fit, we would go to our old high school hangout, sit in our car in the parking lot out back and wait for the carhops on roller skates to bring us an order of French fries and cokes. That was our big night out! I knew we were saving money to build our own home. But what we weren't building were memories that would keep this relationship special. I yearned for more from this man that I had married — more dinners out, more special evenings together, more conversation, more romance. But those things were not embraced as important by me when choosing a mate. Instead, I chose from my little-girl need to feel safe and secure.

I share these facts with you because I feel it is important to understand how society worked back in the 1960's and 70's in case you, the reader, are the age of my children and grandchildren. What I was taught as acceptable behavior was very different than what I see now. It's important to my story to understand what was going on in my mind during those years. I became so co-dependent with man1, that I no longer knew who I even was. Things are a little different today. At least that is my hope. Looking back now and seeing how things changed, I am appalled at myself for taking on so many responsibilities and never speaking out. But this is the way I grew up. I simply traded one authority figure, my parents, for another — man1. This is how I thought all relationships worked. This was how a woman was taken care of. Today, I hope women are smarter and stronger than I ever was. And this way of thinking certainly helps to explain why I reacted as I did when future events took place.

Man1 called me Peepee. That was his nickname for me because he said I was such a skinny little girl. I think now it was also his way of reminding me that I was not as strong as he was, and I would need him to take care of me. I remember his mother coming to our apartment before we got married to teach me how to iron his clothes. She even showed me how to iron his underwear. That I never did. Guess, even for me, there had to be a line somewhere. I remember, while riding in the car driving to Florida to see his parents, I would mend the holes in his work socks. I never wrote a check until over ten years into this marriage. If I wanted a new dress, I was allowed to go shopping but I couldn't make a purchase. I was to take man1 back to the store with me so he could see the dress on me and he would decide if I was allowed to have it. If the answer was "yes", he would write the check or use his credit card.

I remember going to the county fair one year with him. After walking around a bit, I asked if I could have something to eat. A candied apple would be great. Upon finding out how much they cost, he decided it was too much money and I left without the only thing I really wanted. I wasn't worth even the price of a candied apple.

All these small judgments on his part were hurtful. But because I had been raised in a home where I felt judged, criticized, and found wanting most times, it was all very "normal" to me. On the outside, I seemed to weather the storms fairly well. On the inside, my list of resentments was growing longer by the day.

Financially we did well together. I'll give you that. Within two years of our marriage we built our first duplex. The Vietnam War continued, and it was around this time the government began drafting married men but not fathers. Lo and behold — my husband decided this would be a good time to start a family.

CHAPTER 10

BEFORE THE BABIES came, I continued to work at the same company where I had been hired right out of high school. And after a one-year stint in the steno pool and another year as secretary to the Asst. Office Manager, I was placed in the executive offices. Before I was offered this job, I was told, "We'll promote you, if you don't plan to get pregnant right away." Hopefully, that cannot be said any longer. But then I was working at a time in the 1960's when women had to wear dresses or skirts to work. No trousers for us! It was just part and parcel of how women were seen and treated in those days. We were really never a whole person. I think we were treated as an adjunct to the men in this very patriarchal society.

I was excited to be the youngest executive secretary the company ever had. Unfortunately, I soon discovered it wasn't that thrilling after all. I dusted my boss's desk every morning and every lunch time. I brought him coffee when he came into the office in the morning. My boss traveled a lot and was gone from the office for weeks at a time. After cleaning out and reorganizing files, desk drawers, credenza files, anything I could get my hands on, I found that no one really cared what I did as long as I didn't bother anyone else. So I read books — and I wrote poetry. This is when and where I wrote many of the poems

I've kept from the mid to late 1960's. Writing gave me the outlet I needed for the despondency and melancholy I was feeling at that time. Regretfully, I was not even aware then of how out of touch I was with my intuitive nature. I didn't recognize the disconnect. I wasn't even aware of how unhappy I was.

I shared a poem I wrote back then with my co-worker, another executive secretary with whom I shared an office. Upon reading it, she just looked at me rather puzzled and said, "But how can you feel this way? You're a married woman now."

"Oh, it's not about me." I replied. "It's just something I wrote. It could be about anyone." The irrationality of that statement was blinding. But I didn't see it. I share this poem with you now so you can see, as I have finally recognized, the deep disconnect between my inner and outer self.

TO MATURITY

My body is restless —
Wishing for Maturity —
Yet afraid of the uncertainties to come.
Longing for Love —
A real and physical love between two people.
Aching to be free —
To be master of my feelings and desires.

My Mind is restless —
Longing for knowledge —
To know all of life and love there is to know.
Unwilling to remain quiet —
I toss at night and try to sort my thoughts.

My Soul is restless —
Looking for an Answer —
To the profound and exciting question of life.

Searching for Peace —
An inward peace of all my being.

I am Restless.
Body, Mind and Soul.
Confused, forlorn and lost.
Yet looking, longing, for the day
When light will dawn and I will see
A world I never saw before.

This shows perfectly my state of mind at this time. I just wasn't really plugged into much of my life at all. On the outside, things looked fairly normal, however, on the inside I was fading away. Part of me kept saying I should be happy because I had someone to take care of me. I had that authority figure I so thought I needed to help me make good decisions. Another part of me crawled into a cave and wanted to die.

I worked at that particular job for three years. Finally I received my five-year company pin and quit, pregnant, that same week. I learned from the other women working there that you never told your boss your correct due date. The bosses really didn't want you working when your baby belly was showing. So most due dates were about a month or two off. Thus my days of working outside my home were over, at least for the next seven years.

We had three beautiful children in three-and-a-half years. We built our second duplex and moved in. We were at last living the American Dream.

CHAPTER 11

EVERYTHING LOOKED PRETTY on the outside. We were a young, church-going family, daddy holding down a proper job and mommy staying home with the children. We had a new house and a new car. We were certainly on our way. I had found a rut in which I could feel comfortable — not happy — but comfortable. Circumstances were certainly similar to what I had always been accustomed to — that of giving up my authority to another.

It was just so darn easy to allow someone else to be in charge. Tell me what to do. Tell me where to go. Tell me how to be. Fix it for me. Do it for me. Say it for me. So easy, so comfortable not to be responsible. Being married and a mother does not make one a grownup.

I believe my awakening began about this time as I had accomplished those things I thought I wanted most. I had a husband who made good money, three beautiful, healthy children, and a new house to turn into a home. But I was miserable. I felt alone and empty. Those tapes of old kept telling me I should be grateful. I could never survive on my own with three kids. That I would never make enough money with my skills. That I could never stand the rigors of being both breadwinner and home-maker for my children and myself.

During this period I had many recurring dreams of being chased by bad people. I wore myself out running and hiding and always getting caught. The dreams always frightened me and I would wake up heart pounding, out of breath, wild-eyed and wondering WHY. I have come to find out that these dreams are very common when caught in the turmoil of living an inauthentic life. A life that does not reflect the truth of who you really are.

I vividly remember choosing a book to read so different from my typical mystery/romance novels that I felt sure the book had actually chosen me. It was called How I Found Freedom in an Unfree World by Harry Browne. To me in my beginning throes of birthing my true Self, I found this book fascinating, revolutionary, and mind opening. The ideas, to me in my naïveté, were new and exciting. Ideas like: You are always responsible for your own thoughts and actions. If you are unhappy with where you are in your life, understand that every choice you made to get you here was yours. You are not a victim.

These were new ideas to me. For the first time in my life I began to feel truly empowered. The acceptance of the idea that I had, indeed, chosen my lot in life was actually very freeing. For along with that knowledge came the following truth — that I could now make different choices.

This was a very revolutionary idea for me as I had always felt myself a prisoner to my past. If only I hadn't married so young. If only I didn't have three children. If only I had gone to college. If only... whatever — my life would be different. I was always the victim. This new knowledge turned on its head all I had believed true for myself.

Thus, I began an inward journey to Self. Oh, I still did my life topside, and to most people I suppose it still looked like it always had — happy housewife, mother, and church activities' volunteer. But underneath were the smoldering coals now ready to ignite a fire big enough to burn away the lies I had been living.

There followed about three years of inner searching, trying out some of my newly found courage. Then one day as I sat deliberately making lists of why I should leave and why I should stay in this marriage, a most amazing thing happened. I had consciously decided that it would be so much better (translate that as "easier") for me to stay with my children's father until my youngest child was eighteen years old. That would mean staying another fourteen years. I wouldn't be that old. And at that time I could begin anew, still young enough, pretty enough, and good enough to start all over again. Yet, just as I mentally made that choice, there flashed through my body a vision I shall never forget. I instantly saw myself looking in the mirror on that long-awaited day of my daughter's eighteenth birthday. Looking back at me was what I perceived as an ugly, old woman, more witch than wonderful.

Immediately I knew I would never survive another fourteen years lived like the last fourteen. I knew I HAD to leave and go as quickly as possible. Something deep inside me knew it could not remain buried any longer.

So I began to make plans to leave my safety net, my security, my home, risking family ties and broken friendships. There was no conscious choice to make. For deep within the limits of my darkly buried psyche was that one small spark which for a briefest moment flamed brightly white and seared a knowing from my Soul to all my being — the time to leave is NOW.

I always thought what I saw staring back at me from my mirror that day was just an older, used up version of my outer self. What I've come to understand is that what I was so privileged to glimpse was what some would call my Baba Yaga, my wild woman, my wizened witch. I choose to call her my Soul. What the message really meant was not that if I stayed I would grow old, but that if I stayed I would not learn to know the real me.

And thus, my writing changed. From rhyming verse about clouds and kids, I began writing free verse about what I was feeling and the changes I was experiencing. I preserved and kept safe these cherished writings, even including them in a book I put together for my children in 1999 called <u>Just Me</u>. I wanted them to know me as a person, not just their mother. Little did I know how consequential these writings would be in opening long-closed doors that would literally shine a light on the person whom I had begun to be.

THE EVENT

CHAPTER 12

My divorce from man1 was final on March 1, 1976. It was now February, 1977, and it was cold. Snow lay on the ground covering lawns and shrubbery leaving the roads and walkways clear. It was shortly after midnight and my children and I were sleeping soundly, each in our own beds, in our own rooms. Slowly, I began to awaken, becoming aware that someone was in bed with me.

Sometimes the body can betray. Until my mind awoke enough to understand what was taking place, this is exactly what happened. What he was doing felt good. More than that I do not know. It was at about this point I began waking up — first to a fleeting feeling of excitement which turned quickly to confusion and then just as quickly to full-out panic. Gripped by a fear that was almost palpable and a terror that made rational thinking impossible, I opened my eyes, realizing I had not gone to bed with anyone. I should have been alone.

My first panicked thought, when I realized there was a stranger in my bed, was "Don't kill me!" I looked for a weapon. Did he have a gun, a knife? Would this be a struggle for my life? I knew what he wanted, and I felt helpless to save myself. I saw no weapon, but my fear also screamed that he was bigger and stronger than I was. That struggling would lead to more danger and probably injury. He seemed to be fully dressed and stank of cigarettes.

My heart was pounding in my ears. I moved in a fog. I felt like this was a dream. I couldn't believe this was actually happening. "Who are you? How did you get in?" That's all I can remember saying over and over. The intruder calmly replied that I had let him in. Each time I asked that question, that was his reply. He said my sliding glass door in the family room was standing open and that's how he had come in. I just remember saying over and over that I hadn't let him in. I know I was whining and half crying. I was too afraid to be angry.

I must have been causing him some problems. Maybe I was talking too loudly. Maybe I was being combative. I know I just kept asking "How did you get in?" Finally he grabbed me by the arm and shoved me down the hall to the family room. There, indeed, my sliding glass door stood wide open, the cold air blowing the flimsy draperies into the room.

He pushed me onto the floor and got on top of me. I must have had my eyes closed because all I can remember is how terrible he smelled. I may have been crying. I may have been yelling. Maybe I was even fighting. I just don't remember. The next thing I do remember is my eight-year-old son coming into the room yelling at me because there was a man in our house. He had appointed himself my protector and guardian since his father was no longer living with us.

As my son scolded from the doorway, the intruder calmly got up and walked out that open door onto a small wooden balcony and down the steps to the ground. Footprints in the snow were later seen from those steps across my front yard to the street.

I had to remain calm. Had to remain in charge. I closed and locked that sliding door, already feeling stupid and guilty for not having a piece of wood in it. Obviously, I had made a mistake and something awful had happened. I quieted my son and got him back to bed. Then I looked around. How could I go back to bed? I couldn't go back into that room and that bed where it all had started. But who could I ask for help.

CHAPTER 12

It seemed like everything was happening in slow motion. Nothing felt real. Counseling since has taught me there are actually three possibilities when trauma occurs — fight, flight or freeze. This makes so much sense to me now and knowing this could have saved me so much pain and heartache later on. I froze. I didn't fully remember what had happened. The event is remembered through a fog.

Not knowing what else to do, I called a friend who was a city patrol officer. In my remembrance, I remained very calm. He later told me that I was so hysterical when I called that he had his wife keep me on the telephone until he arrived at my house. I explained to him what had happened. He asked me if I had been raped. I didn't want to appear stupid, but I had to be truthful. I told him I didn't know. I said the intruder did not finish what he started because my son had interrupted him. So I didn't know if you would call it rape or not. He patiently explained to me that any penetration is considered rape. "Then yes," I conceded, "I had been raped."

I'm not sure what I thought would happen but it certainly wasn't what happened next. He told me that unfortunately he couldn't do anything for me because my house lay outside the city limits. Just across the street from me, the houses were inside the city limits. I would have to call the county sheriff's department to handle this. I think he realized how difficult it would be for me to make another call and tell this story once again. He called them for me.

I had already decided that there was no way I was going to subject myself to any further degradation by going to the hospital for a rape exam, especially since the rapist hadn't finished what he'd started. Besides, it was widely known, especially during that time, that in cases of rape, the victim was more often than not put on trial herself. I couldn't allow that to happen. I was a single woman who went out on alternate weekends when my children were visiting their father overnight. I danced and drank and enjoyed the company of many friends, both male and female. I was already considering the possibility that whoever had come to my home may have seen me out somewhere and followed me home. So obviously, what happened was caused by my choices and my carelessness. I'm sure I wasn't really thinking straight at the time. But I'm sure, too, as a young mother recently divorced, I did not want to put myself or my children through any kind of public humiliation which pressing charges could have created.

Two deputies came to my home, and I had to relate all over again what had happened to me. They listened and were kind. They asked me enough questions to fill out their forms, disappointed that I would not agree to go to the hospital. But they understood my hesitancy. They told me a detective would contact me the next day to get more information. They left. My friend insisted that my children and I come to his house for the remainder of the night. I didn't want to go, but I didn't want to stay at my house either. So I went, glad that I had someone taking care of me and telling me what to do.

The next day I called off work. I phoned the man I had been dating to tell him what had happened. Of course, he was sorry and rushed to my side to comfort me and stay with me. In the afternoon the detective came to my house to fill out his report. He was much less than kind. He made it very clear to me that even if this rapist was caught, because I was unwilling to go to the hospital, there would be no proof that what I said was true. I understand his frustration with me. I wish he could have understood how embarrassed, humiliated, and guilty I felt. My boyfriend at the time was concerned that the intruder might come back since he hadn't finished what he'd started. I shared this concern with the detective who assured me that they never had a case on record where a rapist came back. Since that time, I have found that statement to be entirely false.

Because my boyfriend was concerned for my safety, he insisted on staying over at my house, sleeping on the couch. It drove me crazy having someone there and underfoot constantly. I had just begun to find my way to a more emotionally mature young woman, and I felt that I was giving up so much of the freedom that I had recently won.

After a couple of weeks, things calmed down to the point where

CHAPTER 12

you could say we were functioning almost as usual again. My boyfriend stopped spending every night with me. That couldn't have gone on indefinitely any way. The only occurrence that was out of the ordinary was that I was receiving quite a few hang-up phone calls. Like I said previously, my intuitive radar wasn't working well yet. I was just beginning to learn to listen and believe what my inner instincts were telling me. This one didn't even register.

Most things had gone back to normal. However, I wasn't sleeping well at all. Six weeks to the day later, I opened my eyes to see that silhouette in the doorway of my bedroom. He was back! This time I was immediately wide awake. I knew what he wanted and I was not going to give in. Since I'm a talker, not a fighter, I thought I could engage him in conversation and change his mind about what his intentions were. Yeah, great thinking! Like that was ever going to happen. But I tried.

I was frightened, but more than that, I was furious. He had come back and I was told that wasn't going to happen. "How did you get in?" I angrily asked.

"Same way I did last time." He calmly answered, almost smiling as he said it.

"No you didn't" I countered. "I put a piece of wood in that door. I know you didn't come in that way."

He laughed. "I didn't come in that way last time either. I came in through the garage, into the basement and up the stairs to the hall."

"But those doors to the garage and basement are locked!" I argued.

Laughing again, he replied "I can get through any lock except a deadbolt. Right now your front door is standing wide open in case I have to leave quickly."

Once again, I had been short-sighted and stupid. I was almost as angry with myself as I was with this intruder. I felt deflated and defeated. Since I knew I could never win if a physical altercation took place, I felt if I could keep him talking, he wouldn't be doing anything else. So talk I did. I remember purposefully getting out of bed and going to the window in that darkened bedroom. I cautiously moved the curtain away from the window to allow more moonlight into the room so I could get a better look at his face. I figured if he was going to finish what he'd started, I was at least going to get a good look at him and be able to describe what he looked like. I saw that he was fully dressed. A young white man, built short and rather husky. He was fully clothed with a knit cap pulled over his hair.

As we moved in almost a slow-motion dance around my bedroom, I felt I could probably make a run for it since I knew my front door was standing open. However, in order to do that, I would have had to leave him in the house with my children. That I would not do. If he had hurt one of them, I would never have been able to live with myself. I stayed in the room with him. All these thoughts played out in my disheartened head as I tried to keep him focused on anything except that for which he had come.

I kept asking him why he was doing this. All he would say was that he loved me. "This isn't something you do to someone you love." I begged, all pretense of bravado gone. He didn't see it as hurting me at all. He told me he had been watching me. How he would sit outside that sliding door on my little balcony outside my family room and watch through those flimsy drapes. My stomach dropped. How dare he invade my privacy like that. How dare he intrude on my personal moments in that way. That act in itself is also a form of rape. Now I knew why those hang-up calls had happened. He was checking to see if I was home. Earlier that evening, my boyfriend had received a hang up call also. Checking, I'm sure, to make sure he wasn't at my house. I was angry once again and afraid all at the same time. I wanted to scream and yell for help but was afraid it would only anger him further. I felt a total inability to control anything that was happening to me.

When he grew tired of the word games we seemed to be playing, he decided it was time to get on with what he had come for. I had done the one thing I thought might be a deterrent — keep him talking. Obviously, that hadn't worked. So by this time I just wanted it to be over with. I had read somewhere years before that whatever a woman does to survive a rape is the correct thing to do. Sometimes if a woman fights, it only makes her rapist angry and more damage is done. So I turned off my mind and allowed him to do with my body what he wished. He actually became upset and scolded me because I wasn't emotionally participating in his act of self gratification and control.

When he was finished, he tucked me into bed, pulling the covers up under my chin. "I love you," he whispered. "Now you can take a shower or a bath or whatever you need. I'm leaving. I'll close and lock your front door." He said it as if I had invited him over for the evening.

I listened for the front door to close. I felt totally defeated. Desolate, afraid and helpless, I shakily got out of bed and went to the telephone. The first call I made was to the Rape Crisis Center. I hesitantly told the woman who answered that I had been raped. The first words she said to me were to ask me my name. I hung up. I'm not sure why I chose to make the next call, probably because I was desperate for an understanding voice. Even though it was after midnight, I called the office of the psychologist I had talked with about my divorce. I really never thought about how late the hour was, but as fate would have it, he was still in his office. Or perhaps he had his calls forwarded to his home. I'm not sure which it was and I didn't ask. He came over to my house and I told him what had happened — about both times the intruder broke into my home. I told him I didn't want to call the police. After all, they're the ones who told me it wouldn't happen again. He asked me if I would feel better if he looked through my house to make sure there was no one there. I told him yes. So he meticulously checked all the rooms, all the closets, all the doors, the basement and the garage to make sure there was no one in my house. When he was sure I was safe, he left. The next day he sent a man over to my house to install deadbolt locks on my front door and on the door in the hallway leading to my basement. I chose that door because the utility doors into both the garage and the basement were so cheap. I was afraid those doors could be pushed in or knocked down too easily. Plus, I would have had to remember every night to lock that door and I was afraid to go into the basement and garage. Of course, that became just one more reason for me to feel stupid and guilty. There had never been a lock on the door at the top of those basement steps, and it could easily be locked before bedtime. I will forever be so grateful to that wonderful therapist for the care and kindness he showed me.

The next day, too, I called that detective who so cavalierly told me that they had no record of any rapist ever returning. "Well now you have!" I informed him. I even called a counselor I had heard of who dealt specifically in sexual assault cases. I explained over the phone what had happened to me. I described what this rapist had done and the things he had said to me. I asked if there was some other way I could have dealt with him. I was torn apart inside knowing that he said he loved me. Fearing that he would come back again. I believed that whatever a woman does to survive being raped is right. I was afraid to fight and yet knew I couldn't just give in if it were to happen again. The counselor assured me that I had handled the situation as well as could be expected. He said the perpetrator sounded like a psychopath and that fighting with him might have only angered him and would have made him more dangerous. But I knew in my heart of hearts, I couldn't just let it happen again.

Then two weeks to the day, he came back. But this time there was a lock on that door at the top of the basement steps. A lock where before there had been nothing.

That was the most frightening time of all for me, as I lay curled in a ball beside my bed waiting for the sheriff's department to answer my call, knowing who stood on the other side of that door. Thank God, there was now a deadbolt lock there.

It seemed minutes before my call was answered, and I was told a squad car would be sent to my home. I waited at least twenty minutes for them to come. By the time they got there, everything was quiet, closed and locked up. Even though I was relieved when they got there, I was irritated because I know they didn't believe me that someone tried to break into my home again. They tried to tell me that because both the garage and basement doors were locked, there had never been an intrusion. I know better. I heard the door jiggle at the top of the stairs. I saw the light come on under the door. The rapist had come into my house again the way he had the first two times, garage door to basement door and up the stairs to the hallway. But this time there was a deadbolt lock on that door. That's why I heard the door shake in its frame as he jiggled the knob to open it. That's why I saw the light go on under the door when he flipped the switch to see why he couldn't enter as he had before. It doesn't surprise me at all that he would have locked the doors behind him when he left. The deputies who came out that night even told me to call a neighbor next time as a neighbor would get there before they could. I felt they were done dealing with me.

THE AFTERMATH

CHAPTER 13

I DIDN'T WANT to talk about what happened. I told very few people, only those whom I felt had to know. The only family member I shared this with was my sister. I never went into details. In fact, this writing is the first time ever I have forced myself back to those events to put it all into written form. I had talked with a counselor, but that for me was much different than actually reliving the events and memorializing them on paper. This has made it all so much more real than I ever wanted it to be. But I know, too, that in the telling, in the yelling and the crying, lie the healing of that wound that still cries out for wholeness.

I had drawn a sketch of his face, from what I could remember from that second visit, and gave it to both the sheriff's department and city police department. I don't know if he was ever arrested or not. I looked over my shoulder constantly while going about my normal day-to-day activities. I jumped at loud noises. I thought I saw his face everywhere I went. I found myself in tears many times for apparently no reason at all. I couldn't sleep because every time I closed my eyes at night I thought I saw him standing in my doorway. When I did finally fall asleep, I had nightmares.

The man I had been dating when all this occurred eventually asked me why I didn't fight when it happened. I stopped seeing him shortly after that. To be honest, there were many times I wished that the disgrace could have been seen on the outside. I thought if I had been shot or stabbed or beaten black and blue that somehow it would have been better. Somehow the pain would show. When the wounds are carried only on the inside and not seen by others, it may make the shame and guilt easier to carry there, too. And it all became something I did to myself.

I would react viscerally when seeing a story on the TV screen or hearing on the radio about a woman who had suffered sexual abuse. My heart hurt. My stomach turned. My head pounded. My eyes teared up and it was difficult to swallow. At first I avoided all programs that might lead to these reactions. Later, I felt strangely drawn to reading about them.

I was given a gun to protect myself. It was a small handgun, I think a .22 caliber. I kept it under my pillow in my bed so I would have it at night. Since I don't really like guns, I made the decision never to have a loaded gun in the house. So even though the gun was in my bed, the clip was in the top drawer of my dresser. I didn't want the gun, but I thought it might stop the nightmares I was having. It all seemed like a grand idea until the night I woke up sitting up in my bed holding that gun, pointing it right at the open doorway. It wasn't loaded, but what if it had been! And what if one of my children had come into my bedroom during the night and I thought it was the intruder again. And here I was holding a gun! That was the end of having a firearm in the house. I gave it back to the owner.

I was taking night classes at our local college. I vowed that I would not allow this sick individual to take anything more from me. So I continued attending classes. The walk to and from my car in the student parking area was almost painful. I fast-walked, almost ran from car to building and then from building to car. I looked for other students who were entering or leaving when I was and tagged along with them so I wasn't alone.

I only missed one day of work. Other than refusing to speak about what happened, I'm sure it all may have looked like normal behavior to others, but I assure you there was nothing "normal" about any of it. All those fearful, limiting thoughts and feelings that had so plagued me while growing up were back again — in spades! I began, once again, to believe I just couldn't take care of myself. That left to my own devices, I would make horrible decisions and put myself and my children in danger. Unfortunately, I was not aware of just how deep and ugly this wound to my soul would be and how long it would remain buried and unhealed, running my life and feeding my fears.

THE MIDDLE YEARS AFTER

CHAPTER 14

So there it was. That thing that happened that was so out of sync with the rest of my life. It was a trauma that didn't fit. So I never tried to make it relevant. I just wanted to forget about it.

When I resolved that this stranger would not take anything more from me than he already had, I had no idea then just how much I would give up.

So I simply stuffed the experience down and out of sight. I buried it deep inside me where I thought no one, not even me, would ever have to deal with it again. I remember a very short conversation I had with my sister, one of a very few people who knew what had happened. She asked me if I was angry about someone breaking into my home and raping me. She asked, I guess, because I had never expressed anger to her about it. My answer speaks volumes for where my head and heart had gone. "No" I answered. "He's obviously a very sick man for having done what he did. So how can I be angry with him."

Unfortunately, I just quietly and sadly slipped back into that oh-so-comfortable place for me where I knew I couldn't take care of myself, just as I had done most of my life. I believed down deep inside myself, a place so deep I was not even aware it existed, that all that happened was somehow my fault. I chose to get divorced. I chose to live alone with my children. I didn't have the proper locks on my doors. I was a single woman whom he may have seen out somewhere. I couldn't get angry because I carried around all the guilt for what had happened. The thoughts in my head kept telling me that I had made a big mess of things when I was in charge. I believed once again what my upbringing and all of society taught me: I needed a man to take care of me. So I crawled back into my shell and looked for my knight in shining armor. I returned to that place that said all that mattered was following the rules, looking pretty, being pleasing, and never showing anger.

My powers of intuition and self-empowerment were simply not strong enough to support any continuing growth after having experienced the trauma I had. Having buried so successfully the rapes and the lessons I may have learned from that terrifying experience, I had no tools to work with. My toolbox was empty. I simply carried on in life from that place that felt so familiar, that place that said I couldn't take care of myself. That place that said I needed an authority figure to run my show. Someone to make all my decisions for me. I was right back where I had started. Back to the little girl who always screwed things up when left to her own devices.

I attempted to begin the life I wanted to live without even realizing I had given up on any emotional growth that had begun. By burying the trauma itself, I had also buried my feelings, my fears, my anger, and my insights. Without going inside myself to face and conquer those buried demons and face the lessons that experience may have taught me, I simply tried to make the outside look acceptable. I changed jobs, changed men, changed going to church, changed friends, and changed my good girl status. It wasn't always pretty. It wasn't always neat. It wasn't always the better choice. And it was always difficult.

For another 2-1/2 years I toiled on my own, working, raising children, taking night classes at my local college, and being landlord and caretaker of the duplex I owned. These were difficult years, tangled, tense and tiring for me. I look back on those years now and don't know how I did it so great were the obligations to do all and be all. At the rate I was taking college classes, it would take me at least twelve years to get that four-year degree. My job in commission-only sales had become more difficult as prospects dried up and guilt over leaving my children each evening loomed larger. Renters in my duplex came and went and work needed to be done, painting, cleaning, repairing. I was out of the nest and living life on my own. It was exhausting. On a conscious level, I was no longer fearful of someone breaking into my home again. I had managed to stuff that experience down far enough to believe it was over and done with. Unfortunately, my subconscious was still struggling. I didn't sleep well. Too many times when I went to bed and closed my eyes, I would open them with a start believing that I was seeing the silhouette of my rapist in the doorway of my bedroom. Of course, there was no one there, but I just couldn't put that one piece to rest. I lived with that anxiety and didn't share it with anyone.

In 2012, for reasons later explained, I set out to discover how a reasonably intelligent woman like myself could have so unwisely chosen the three men I decided to marry. In the midst of my striving to find my deeper Self, I tired of the task. At least that is what I told myself at the time I first wrote this part of my story in 2012. A deeper, truer understanding came later for me. Yet once this idea was accepted by me, I was easily compelled to accede to the role offered to me in the saga of man2. This role promised me a better life, promised to grant me all I wished for and promised to prove to everyone, including myself, that I could "get it right." If only I had listened to the ringing bells, heeded the waving flags, or run away when aware of my intuitive rumblings, I might have saved myself long years of learning.

So when the gilded carriage came along and said he could paint the trim on my duplex and I wouldn't have to pay someone $500 (which I didn't have), I accepted the ride. There are more ways to pay than just with money.

I moved through a very short courtship to an elopement in Las Vegas, starry eyed, walking on clouds, just being in love. We married on September 5, 1979. My knight in shining armor had arrived to carry me off to wonderland. The only thing it cost me was my Self. But that was a bargain not even asked of me. For I gave my Self up without a fight to someone I thought would watch over me and care for me forever. I traded my soul, my passion, my deep spirit dreams for what my overprotective, fearful nature saw as safety, security, acceptance and love. At last I lived once again in a relationship that would keep me safe and secure, stifled and sorry.

CHAPTER 15

EVEN THOUGH THIS man2 was six years my junior, I bestowed upon him the mantle of the wiser one, the more experienced one and the always-correct one. My intuition, though incredibly correct, was shuttled to a place so deep within me it could be neither seen nor heard. For I had made that unspoken bargain once again: "I shall be what you want and you will take care of me."

Through the reading and study I had done through the years, I knew that within each of us burns a senescent force, an older wiser part of Self which knows what is always in our own best interest. This is what those earliest intuitive feelings will mature into if property sustained. Without nourishment and exercise this seat of wisdom cannot grow and strengthen to take on the mantle of guide and leader for our maturing emotional nature. This feeding of my intuitive nature would be accomplished by listening to it. Heeding its little gut poking urgings. Allowing myself a deep breath and a moment to listen to what I was feeling and sensing from inside myself. These are the practices that help develop a strong and trustworthy force within that could have helped me know what is in my own best interest. Obviously, this most important soul work wasn't done by me, and I missed the signals from inside that would have made my journey much easier.

Too often when this soul work has not been done, when this inner growth has not taken place, we blindly hand over to another outside ourselves the power to tell us what to do, when to do it, and how to do it. Under-developed intuitive abilities will always lead to this transfer of authority to someone other than ourselves. This is why I could so readily and easily give up my power to man2.

I wanted so much to be a part of a family, his family, his community, even his religion, that I changed all things about myself to accommodate what I felt he wanted. I merged myself with him wherever I found a space. But I could not totally conform. The fit I'd hoped to have left cracks and crannies where winds blew cold and uncomfortable around my very psyche. No matter how perfect I tried to be, no matter how diligent were my efforts to fit in, I remained discontented, disillusioned and disheartened. My creative life did not fit in any way with my current circumstances. I loved to read and was told that while he lived life, I only read about it. I loved to draw, but my pictures never meant anything to him because they were of *my* children. I was expected to be productive in very concrete ways. There was just no room for the things that fed my soul. I wrote very little during this initial period of time. I thought it was because I was happy. Now I see that my will to create was simply buried too deeply to surface.

My reading, my writing, my art and my music, the very things that made me uniquely me, I gave up without even a blink. That fearful, over-protective part of my brain was back, stronger than ever, admonishing me that I was lucky to have such a good-looking husband and that I had better allow him to make the rules and run the show and never, never disagree with him if I wanted to keep him in my life. So my mouth was sealed. I remained silent on the outside while hot smothering flames burned away my dreams and intuition on the inside.

Funny that I don't remember much about those years, but then I always did have the capacity to "go numb" or enter my "coma state" when life became too overwhelming. On some deep level I knew it wasn't working for me. I still wasn't living the life my very soul longed for. My opinions weren't asked for nor appreciated, especially when they were contrary to what man2 wished for me.

My enrollment in massage school during this period was totally acceptable, even encouraged, since it was initiated by someone man2 respected and liked and eventually would afford me a way to make money. I really didn't want to do it, but felt pushed into it by people and circumstances around me. Now, I am grateful that became my path.

When one loses touch with those inner urging, those intuitive stirrings that tell us how to find our truth, when to stand up and speak out, and which way to go, we enter a state of numbness, not calm. We become depressed, not at peace. And sad, not simply silent. And although I functioned in my outside world quite effectively, I was, underneath it all, gasping for breath while helplessly giving up my soul. Damn it! I had allowed myself to be tamed and trapped once again.

There was a breakthrough for me eight years after "the event" while I was married to man2. I was enrolled in massage school and life seemed to be going fairly smoothly. I had just finished reading a book by Jack Olsen called <u>Son, a Psychopath</u> <u>and His Victims</u>. The book was interesting and insightful. But what mattered to me was my reaction when I finished reading it. My first thought as I closed the book was "It wasn't my fault." That's when I realized I had been carrying around for the past eight years all the guilt and shame for what had happened to me.

After several months of anxiety attacks, I called the Rape Crisis Center once again. This time I was ready to talk to someone. One of the ways anxiety attacks manifest for me is instant tears. One moment I am okay and the next moment I'm crying. I knew it had something to do with the rape, but I didn't know what. So I made that phone call.

The young woman I went to see, whose name I unfortunately do not recall, spent almost two hours with me. She listened quietly while I described to her what I'd been through. She assured me that it was not unusual at all for someone to come forward eight years after the assault. That it takes that long to begin processing it and be able to speak about it. She asked if I had told my parents. I said no. She asked me if they were loving and nurturing. I said no. She told me then there was no need at all to tell them if I didn't want to. So I didn't. It took me another two years to feel comfortable enough to do so. And even then, I only told my mother. The counselor just wanted me to feel safe. She asked me if I had told my children. I said no. She suggested if I felt safe doing so, it might be a good time as my kids were in high school and the Rape Crisis Center was doing programs there about date rape. So finally, one-by-one, I told my children.

As an outgrowth of that conversation with my daughter, she invited me to participate in one of her classes at high school. This one-semester class taught students about living in the real world, about dealing with real feelings, and facing challenges presented by actual life circumstances. The class was interested in speaking with someone who had experienced fighting in the Vietnam war and someone who had experienced being raped. The purpose was to share the feelings of the person involved, not necessarily the details of the experience itself. My daughter asked me if I would be willing to share with her class. After making sure she was comfortable with my speaking about what happened, I agreed. I don't remember much from that short class I attended. However, I do remember sitting cross legged on the floor with about fourteen students, mostly girls and talking briefly about the break-ins. I shared with the students the feelings of fear, shame, embarrassment and sadness I felt. After my little talk, the teacher suggested we go around the circle and let the students tell me how they felt hearing my story. To my absolute shock, half the girls admitted that they, too had experienced some form of sexual abuse. The boys expressed their sadness that I had to go through what I did. Then the school bell rang. This was a last period class, and all the teenagers jumped up, grabbed their stuff and left the room. It was a very abrupt ending to a most emotional forty-five minutes. But they couldn't miss that big yellow school bus! The next day, I asked my daughter what ever happened after that class. She assured me that the teacher, a very nice young man, had allowed the students to share again the next day about their feelings and put some closure to it. That day was never mentioned again.

The Rape Crisis counselor explained to me that one of the most difficult areas to heal after a trauma like this is that feeling of having no control. She asked me if I was having any recurring dreams. I told her yes I was but the dream didn't have anything to do with being raped. I really couldn't see where this could possibly be helpful. How was a person supposed to gain control over a situation that obviously had already happened and she had no control over it when it did. She asked me what I was dreaming. So I related to her this crazy dream I had experienced about five or six times. It was one of those dreams that seem so real you never forget it. In my dream the ex-wife of man2 brings her children to me and tells me I have to babysit them as she has things she needs to do. I didn't want to do this as I had things I needed to take care of also, but I always begrudgingly agreed to do as I was asked. Two nights after this counseling session, I had that dream again. This time in the dream when his ex-wife stopped by my house to ask me to take care of her children, I stood my ground and told her I was busy and couldn't do it that day. You know how your voice is shaky and breathy when speaking when you're very nervous? That's just what my voice was like in the dream when I began talking to her. I almost couldn't speak. But as I continued telling her that I couldn't do what she asked, my voice got stronger and I felt calmer.

Amazingly, that was the last time I had that dream! I was actually taking back control through that dream. I know it wasn't the same circumstances, but my mind really needed to do some healing and that dream allowed me to do that. Dreams really can be meaningful in our lives. Listen to them. Pay attention to them. I share this because the experience was so astounding. I now do believe that through that dream I took back some of the control I had lost in the event of being raped. I think this, too, is why I thought the healing had been completed at that time. Little did I realize how deeply that wound was buried and how it would still control my life.

CHAPTER 16

I knew something was very wrong with my life because I was angry so much of the time. Not in an assertive "state your problem" kind of way but rather in a very passive/aggressive "throw the dish and tell you what a jerk you are" kind of way. The entire period of attending massage school, working part-time, studying, mothering, wifing, and home making bred in me not peace and acceptance but an anxiety-driven search for that which just might make me happy. I joined with several other women to begin a support group. I realigned with my sister, to spend more time with her. Our friendship had suffered during this marriage as man2 felt that our visits together were keeping me from getting done the things I needed to do for him and my children. I cringe at my inability to speak up when I look back on that particular time. I made a few new friends and many more acquaintances. Yet, my cup remained empty. I finally figured out that I needed to stop searching outside myself and go within to reclaim those parts I had once again given up.

This was also a time when I started having another recurring dream. In this dream, I was lost in some huge building, usually a school or hospital, looking for a particular room that I never could find. Another dream that occurred often which I enjoyed immensely, was of a home we had purchased. It was quite large, and although it had two stories, we lived only on the bottom floor. When I would proudly show people around my house, they would be very impressed with its size and design. I would tell them that they hadn't seen anything yet. "Just wait until I show you what's upstairs." And up the steps we would go to an unbelievable space of beautiful rooms, comfy, cozy nooks and spacious bathrooms. Everything was laid out in a way that there were always "surprise" rooms at the end of a hall, or rooms that would go on and on and then end in one of those wonderful, zany bathrooms. It was a palace, a retreat, inviting, spacious and beautiful. Everyone would ask me why we never lived in these rooms. I usually replied that either I didn't know or that we had to fix them up. I loved this particular dream as I always felt I was seeing something good and special about my home. Now I understand that I was really seeing those undiscovered, undeveloped parts of my own psyche.

When a person loses all authenticity, when one's greatest dreams, artistic endeavors, and soul seeking journey are buried so deeply in the shadow they are not even recognized as lost, there is no other alternative but that a new personality is created. A secret life is born from the barren fields of a loveless existence.

I remember with sadness how tamed and fearful I had become in my marriage with the gilded cage — man2. So afraid was I of not being accepted (loved) by him that we never had even so much as a disagreement for the first four years of our marriage. If someone told me that now, I would believe one of them was holding back. And, of course, in this relationship, that one was always me. I allowed him to make rules for not only me but my children, too. How sad for all of us that my strength, my belief in my own power and wisdom had sunk so deeply into my inner workings that I didn't even remember how to call them up any longer. No wonder the anger came bubbling up like geysers of hot steam and slop to overflow periodically and cause those around me to wonder if I still had all my faculties.

How sad that I felt a need to hide my deck of cards under the couch and turn off the television when I heard his car in the driveway. I would dive into the kitchen and try to look as if contemplating what to fix him for dinner was what I had just been doing. I sneaked playtime for myself like that. I sneaked time with girlfriends shopping, talking, and having coffee. I sneaked cigarettes. I sneaked writing at the park and crying in the car. And, finally, I sneaked a lover.

Sneaking isn't healthy. It goes against all that our inner Selves know as truth. Yet if one buries so deeply the very traits that make one who she really is, then why would we be surprised that their very essence should boil up inside to eventually ooze out and stain the falsely perfect life we've made for ourselves and others on the outside.

That's exactly what always happens when we ignore, forget, disregard or neglect our deep Self work. We try to fill those gaping holes with things on the outside —material objects, addictive habits, bad behaviors — all things we're really not.

Where had that brave, young woman gone who wrote those powerful poems about finding something beautiful and lasting inside herself? She'd lost it all again. I didn't even know it was gone. I was gone.

Deception will always exact its own price. Sooner than later the jig will be up, the show will be over and the roll of the "good times" will end. The truth shall set you free — even if it hurts. It took me only a couple months to realize that the lesson I was learning was that once again I had become trapped in my outside life. I wasn't living my authentic life. I was not honoring my most inner desires for creativity, expression and love. I was still shackled to the belief that I needed someone else to hold me up, hold my hand, lead me on, and lead me to my most perfect life — that one lived from the inside out. Unfortunately, I had not developed my inner psyche enough to understand that what I really needed was to hold OUT until I alone could and would find what was most healthy and meaningful for me. Was I not the only one who really knew what that life would look like? Of course, without honoring and including all the pieces of my life, this was impossible for me to do at this time. So I did what I always did — I blamed myself.

CHAPTER 16

This made it easy for me to think that I could not do on my own what I needed to do to be free to follow my dreams.

So with the knowledge that this second marriage was not much different from my first, I once again made plans to leave my home. This time, however, I thought it was different. Funny how the same lesson can show up in so many varied ways. So diverse that I wasn't savvy enough to catch on to the rerun of the same old drama. I thought things were different because this time I wasn't alone in leaving. I had man3 who pledged on bended knee, with tear-filled eyes, with fervid touch, and histrionic pleading that he would always be there for me and I would never be unhappy again. WOW! Did that sound like something I wanted to sign up for!

Now looking back, I remember when I introduced this lesson (read man3) to my mother, for the first time, at a very public place. He leaned down and kissed her and said these very words, "You'll never have to worry about Joanne again. I'll take care of her." My mother's reaction was one of surprise, which she later described to me as "shock." I, however, smiled demurely and played my part convincingly, even if deep stirrings made my tummy rumble with discomfort. One can have two working eyes and still be blind.

This was just to be a short dance and then I would be off to do what my heart and soul desired. Oh, little did I know or understand how quickly and completely dreams can disappear.

CHAPTER 17

So once more I left a relationship that I thought would last forever. One that I thought would keep me safe and protected. I left a home I'd helped to build and bless and furnish. Left a house that provided shelter for my body and nothing for my soul. I left a "dream" home in the country. Certainly not MY dream, yet still a beautiful, expensive home if those things are measured in terms of land and wood and bricks and tile.

I remember crying the day my sister and I moved those final belongings of mine from the grand house on the hill to my little two-bedroom apartment in the city. As soon as the tears started, my sister stopped dead in her tracks, looked at me with apprehension and asked a little breathlessly, "Why are you crying?"

"I'm sad" I replied "for all the dreams that are gone. Sad because the life I thought I'd have did not materialize." "OK." she said, relieved that my angst was caused by leaving my anticipated outcomes and not the gilded carriage (man2). Big, big difference in the two.

I never missed the fancy fine house on the hill. But I also fought hard to get what was mine in the fray. I'd like to say that it was all ME in the fight. And maybe, in spite of having man3 at the ready, it really was mostly ME. I hung tough. I fought hard. I was honest and honorable, determined and firm. In the end, I got all that was mine. And "mine" came in dollars and sense. Man2 and his wife-to-be got the house, but I got my share of its value and furnishings, plus an amount to compensate me for the land and equipment they would need to manage it all. And just as important came room to grow and air to breathe, with joy to share and a reason to laugh and be happy once again. I was proud of myself for having been able to confer with my attorney and to appear in court all by myself. Those were big steps for me even if man3 was hanging out in the wings waiting for me.

I hardly had time to fully exhale the stress and sadness as man3 was beckoning me come to him. It was during my move out that he also made moves. He could see the writing on the wall. I wasn't going to hang around. A sneaky life sucks all the energy and elegance and honesty out of being. It was not a place I felt comfortable in nor did I intend to stay there. So he followed my lead and left his wife and home, too. I never asked for that outcome but neither did I deny it a place in my show. He was not in good health. He suffered from a heart condition that he thought would end his life prematurely. His sister had died from the same diagnosis at the age of forty-one. He wore a back brace and sometimes walked with a cane because of a prior back injury. I think the drama of all these health issues and the very real possibility that he would not live a long time, made this romance just that much more dramatic and intense. I didn't feel I could just walk away. As I told my sister, "How can I leave? I give him hope." (A peek into the unhealthy state of mind from which I still operated.) With me, he had found someone to care for him physically. I thought I had, at last, successfully made that illusive bargain that would grant me a life-long protector. Relationships built on need seldom work out well.

I felt exhilaration at being finally free to pursue the life I'd never had. And at the same time I also felt that life-long fear that somehow I didn't have whatever it takes to make it work. And didn't I owe man3 something? After all, he'd been there for me each step of the way as I navigated through depositions, divorce proceedings and all manner of legal maneuvering.

My instincts, still not quite up to the task, caved in and I accepted a connection, thinking it would be a short one. What if he was different? And what if this time the bargain could be struck? That part of me that cried for safety and security and protection wanted, with all my heart and mind, to believe his words were true. My instincts told me something else. I chose to listen to my heart and once again became a codependent player in someone else's life.

When instincts are injured, we find a way to "normalize" all manner of abnormal behavior. Acts of injustice, destruction, assault are seen as demonstrations of love and protectiveness. Many times over those next several months I was given opportunity after opportunity to see what this relationship might really require. I was given a chance to realize what sacrifices I would have to make, and how I would need to alter my own personality to please my partner. Yet, I always caved in, conked out, coughed up and calmed down whenever confronted with abusive behaviors. I learned slowly, yet willingly, to once again live half a life.

While waiting for our divorces to become final, he asked me to marry him. Since we believed his death to be imminent, we didn't want to wait until our divorces were final, as that could have taken several years. It was also about this time that an incident occurred which proved to me again how foolish I could be and what poor choices I would make if left on my own. One night while working with a colleague, I found myself in a situation that I would later understand to be date rape. At the time, I didn't define it that way. It was a situation I thought I could deal with. My instincts told me to leave but, again, I overrode those feelings thinking I could handle whatever happened. It turned out I couldn't, and I gave in to his insistent machinations, fearful of my well-being if I didn't. Again, I felt the guilt and shame of having allowed something unwanted to be forced on me. This event just added proof that I certainly could never take care of myself. I ran straight back to what I perceived to be my safe place with man3. We planned a romantic commitment ceremony alone in the park at the edge of Lake Erie. We read our own marriage vows, played our favorite song, and exchanged rings.

That part of my psyche that was supposed to grow wiser and stronger, the part that is supposed to look after my unsophisticated child, had fallen asleep. Actually, she never really had a chance. Now I understand how those terribly ugly pieces of my life not only left out, but left totally unacknowledged, would actually drive all my thoughts and behaviors. I'd never learned to fully trust those intuitive messages. So that fearful and over-protective part of my brain held the reins and dictated the path on which I would tread. Since I now believed, once again, that I could not take care of myself, I felt I had no choice but to continue on the journey I had started.

CHAPTER 18

With all that having been said, in the beginning it all felt fine. Although I would caution that "If it seems too good to be true, it probably is." But that is what I thought I wanted. At the time I was running my own very successful Neuromuscular Massage Therapy business. I felt very confident in my abilities as a therapist and loved the work I was doing. Unfortunately, that self assurance didn't show up in my relationship life. So I was all too willing to overlook the seemingly small requests in the beginning — like man3 didn't think I should have any male friends now that we were officially non-officially a couple. He didn't want me taking on any new male clients. We went everywhere together. Did everything together. He held my hand when we walked, when we talked, while riding in the car. He touched me constantly, an arm around my shoulder, a stroke to my hand and arm, rubbing the back of my neck. We had our little rituals we followed — the kiss before leaving and again when returning, the peck of a kiss after he helped me on with my coat. They were cute. People smiled when they observed his tender attentions. What I failed to acknowledge and deal with was the anger and sulkiness he displayed when I forgot my part in one of these rituals. So by overlooking these little mood swings, I could feel good about this relationship. Never had I felt so loved, so cherished, so sought after and so desired. It was in December, 1998, that we were officially married.

Too bad that part of my brain, my guardian force, lay so deeply asleep she was not there to warn me that what I was experiencing wasn't love but ownership and control. Man3's attentiveness to me came not from a place of unconditional love but sprang instead from his sea of insecurities. And my acceptance of these ministrations was exactly the same. Didn't I deserve some happiness? Had I not gone through two barren relationships where I was neither appreciated nor allowed to bloom? Is it no wonder when one's life becomes so sterile we cling to the smallest morsel of anything thrown our way? We accept the crumb never understanding our entitlement is the whole cake.

Crawling became normal. Begging became regular. Thinking through new ways to maneuver and manipulate situations to get what I wanted. Weighing absolutely every word before it's said. All these became an accepted way to live. Just an ordinary, everyday walk on eggshells.

When it became evident that this man3 relationship would last far longer than either of us first imagined, I became a little desperate and suggested that it might be time to renegotiate the terms of our agreement. Nothing changed. The problem was I had lived so long in the desert of my inner being without input, help or suggestion from anything deep within me, that I had no idea what would feed my soul. So much time in captivity had dulled my ability to connect in any way to that which I knew was true and connected to my inner longings. Because it happened slowly, over some period of time, I wasn't even consciously aware of the changes taking place and of my total loss of Self.

Like many others in circumstances such as these, I became an addict. My addiction was codependency. It was that feeling of being taken care of, thus safe and secure. It was to not being alone, thus loved. As with all addictions, it soon became what my life was all about. Nothing was more important, certainly not an unseen inner being. No need was more alluring, no desire more strong than simply to meet the need of my addiction. I overlooked, closed my eyes and ears, stepped aside, stepped back and over anything that might have pointed to the truth. My lips were sealed and even the inside screaming had stopped. Again I lay curled in a corner, paralyzed with fear, knowing something wasn't right in my life and for some reason not being able to figure out what it was or even what had gone wrong.

I did all I knew to do to try and right this sinking ship of a marriage. I insisted on counseling. Man3 saw one on his own and together we tried over the years with three others. Nothing changed. And why would it. I thought he was the problem and he *knew* I was. I nursed him through two bouts of cancer. Spent endless nights in the emergency room at a local hospital. He thought he was having a heart attack. Each time it turned out to be an anxiety attack. He had a defibrillator implanted in his chest to kick-start his heart should it stop beating. We stayed together out of a shared need — he thought he needed me to take care of him and I thought I needed him to take care of me. Neither of us was correct.

I kept thinking there was some way to get through to him, something I could say to make him understand how badly I was hurting and make him realize what I needed from him. After all, he had promised to love me and take care of me for the rest of my life. It never happened. That vision of myself remained constant, me curled up in a corner of my room simply waiting to die. I knew my life wasn't working once again. But this time I was old and tired, worn out, overweight and used up. I could no longer offer a perky young thing to get what I wanted. It seemed time had finally run out and there was nowhere to turn. I needed to get up off the floor and get moving, but I couldn't. I lay paralyzed by fear and broken dreams and a sadness so engulfing I just wanted to die. And I really thought I was going to. I wanted my life to be different but I didn't have the knowledge I needed to make the changes that would have to be made.

Then I heard a name. And I knew it was someone I HAD to meet.

Intuition doesn't die, it simply waits for a breath of air to lift it to the surface. One's survival very often provides that opportunity. Since she was a doctor, it was an appointment easily arranged. She turned out to be the door that would open my way to a new life.

THE LATER YEARS

CHAPTER 19

It was December, 2008, and my life was to change once again. It felt devastating at the time, but what began then was an odyssey to finding the real me — the journey to finding my true spirit. That was the year I was forced to make more changes in my life. Forced down a path I wasn't sure I wanted to take. Forced to begin growing up.

This wonderful doctor asked questions and listened to my answers. She told me she sensed a lot of negative energy coming from me, and if I didn't do something about it, I would become ill. When she asked me if I had ever been abused, I stated that many years ago I had been raped. She was very solicitous and asked if I would mind telling her about it. "Of course not." I replied. "It happened over thirty years ago. So everything is fine."

I commenced a short recitation of those three break-ins at my home those many years ago. The longer I talked, the shakier my voice got. The harder I found it to breathe. The faster my heart raced. When I was finished, she simply asked "Do you think you're over it?"

"Well," I truthfully answered, "up until a few minutes ago, I would have said 'yes'. Now, I don't know."

"I think you need to see a counselor about this." She suggested. She had no one to recommend, and I didn't know of anyone either. I feel certain that the timing wasn't right just then for that to happen. I had other business to finish first.

That one conversation with my intuitively-inspired doctor helped me to open the door which allowed me to see my relationship with man3 for all it really was. I had once again involved myself in an abusive, codependent relationship. Finally, I understood and saw the injury, the lies, the hurt and the neglect that were my present relationship. I was fighting to save something not worth saving.

It will never cease to amaze me how the Universe works in our lives. Just twelve days after that epiphany I found proof of what I had long believed was happening. While I read books, searched the internet and studied at the library to find a way to change and save this relationship, man3 just found a girlfriend.

This fact, known for several years by his children, his family, his co-workers and many others was something he could never admit to me. When I realized the lies, the sneaking, the disrespect and abuse would continue, I chose to end my connection with him.

I will always remember that email not meant for my eyes. I felt no shock, no anger, no sadness for those times and events leading up to this moment had left me so dull and dead inside that I could hardly feel anything at all.

But I wasn't alone. As fate would have it, my son was there, too, so I had someone whom I trusted and knew loved me to share this information. And even though I was feeling rather numb at the time, my son was wise enough to say exactly what I needed to hear. He told me there could be no half-way fix. Whichever road I decided to take, stay or leave, there could be no turning back. And if I chose to leave to begin a new life for myself, I would need to grow a backbone. I knew it would take more than just a backbone. It would take every ounce of courage I could find. I would have to find my voice once again and overcome the fear that had been my constant state of being in order to make the changes that needed to be made to save my own life. I knew, too, that no matter how difficult the task seemed to be, I had to begin it right then and there, one step at a time, to free myself. My sister came once again to help me pack up my life and my belongings and start over again. The divorce from man3 was final in June 2009.

CHAPTER 20

The changes on the outside were swift and easy. The changes on the inside much more important and profound. I had to learn to once again trust all those deeply buried instincts. At first I felt lost and confused. Too many friends both old and new thought I should just start my life all over again. To them it all looked different. I lived in a condo not a house. I drove a new car not an old one. I even moved to live in a different city. But I knew these things were not enough. In fact, they were really nothing to do with my real life and my real Self. And that is the journey I had chosen this time. I would search inside myself for my answers instead of depending on someone else's ideas.

If I hadn't chosen this inward venture to soul and serenity, I would simply have lived another chapter in my life just like all the others. This time that would not happen. My journey to Self was taken in fits and starts and not easily at first. I struggled as always, with that nasty, petty voice inside my head that tried to tell me once again that I couldn't do it by myself. Well, I'd tried it three times letting someone else in charge and it never worked. Now I was ready to try it all a different way. I knew this was just the beginning of my journey. But little did I realize just how far and just how deeply I would have to go to uncover all those lost pieces of my soul.

But first I needed time to collect my thoughts, lick my wounds, cry oceans of tears, and make a plan. All those things take time. It took me a long 2-1/2 years to sort through my fears and my friends and decide which I could live without and which I would choose to deal with. I made many missteps and learned much the hard way as I struggled to find my way back to the real me.

I didn't really understand how difficult the journey back would be — remembering who I really am and re-membering with her. I'd lost so much during those years of capture and captivity. I had to learn how to remain awake and aware. Stop being naive, weak and uninformed. I had to stop caring what other people thought of me. I had to learn to take credit for my own accomplishments. I had to stop being afraid of making mistakes and stop taking myself so seriously.

I believe I had the ultimate pity party for myself during those 2-1/2 years from that visit to my doctor to the beginning steps in the freeing of my soul. I didn't mean to let it last so long. I guess I simply proved that once again that law of attraction always works. For the more negative thinking I did, the more negativity I drew around me. I hadn't learned to embrace any part of myself — inside or out. I hated my fat bloated body, my wrinkled aging face, my dry graying hair. Yep, the mirror doesn't lie. Funny how when you focus solely on the physical, the part that really matters just disappears. I wasn't hearing that still small voice so deep inside that screamed for me to look her way.

By the fall of 2011 I'd pretty much reached into the bottom of the pit and wasn't sure if life here was even what I wanted. But then I got a chance to see if that was really how I felt. There's nothing like a little scare that shows you just how vulnerable your body is and just how quickly the piece with which you play here can be taken out. I had that experience. I now have a tiny metal chip in my left breast where a biopsy was done to check for breast cancer. Fortunately for me, everything was negative and I was given a clean bill of health. That experience turned out to cause the thought that broke the dam that then released the clarion call from my own soul that rising up cried loudly and with love — I want to live!

I knew that life would have to spring from that deepest part of my true Self. My realization was not that I simply wanted my body piece to continue here, but that I wanted to be here now in my own true and authentic Self. Finally I made the choice to take my life into my own hands and through my own feminine intuition, create a life that was just right for me — and right just for me.

CHAPTER 21

ON JANUARY FIRST 2012, I awoke with the thought in my head that I needed to read that book I had read twenty years ago and was never able to give away. "You need Women Who Run With the Wolves," was the message loud and clear. That very day I picked up that book which had been tucked inside a cabinet many years ago gathering dust and almost forgotten — very much like my instinctive nature. Now, at last, the book was opened, the pages read so the words and the message danced triumphantly free. I shall forever be grateful to Dr. Clarissa Pinkola-Estes, PhD, for sharing so much truth and love in this wonderful book. Finding myself in her stories helped me discover how I had lost myself in every relationship I entered into. Believing that I could never take care of myself led me to accepting the truths of others and allowing others to make decisions for me. No relationship can ever complete me. I need to be a complete human being myself. Then I have something to offer someone else. Thus I set out to discover how a smart woman like me got caught up in three dysfunctional marriages.

In retrospect, I can certainly see that after writing my story in 2012, as I recalled it — with all its missing parts — I thought I had finished the task. In reality, I was yet to find that piece that would bring together, and make sense of, the choices I had made. Hard as I tried, I could not go further into my search for my soul. Even after all the reading, writing, tears and epiphanies I had encountered, I was stuck. I now know why it was impossible for me to move forward on my own path. For even though I had teased from hiding many of the beliefs and perceptions which supported events in my story, I still hadn't uncovered the pieces I had buried so well deep within my psyche.

After so much searching and difficult rendering, I felt entitled to a rest. So, in one way or another, I stopped exploring my own deep center. I was content at this point to live with what I had uncovered, even though I knew in my heart of hearts it was not the complete story. Maybe, had I continued my journey inward, I would have found my missing parts. Maybe not. I simply may not have been ready to deal on the outside with what my tortured soul was hiding. All I know is that for the next three years I tried my very best to live a life worthy of what I believed myself to be — a stronger, wiser, braver woman in this world.

At times I made myself proud — like when I went skydiving to celebrate my 70th birthday. At other times I knew I had failed miserably. But always, underneath the attempts both large and small to live a different kind of life, it all felt the same. I am aware now that I was trying to go back to what felt "normal" and comfortable for me. In reality, that "normalcy" of the old me was a deadened, flattened version of who I really was. Certainly nothing to be coveted.

My route to present day involved some back tracking, some repetition, and lots of capitulation. Yet, I can knowingly say that I made headway on my path to maturity. I didn't understand nor bravely honor that intuitive part of myself, but at least I was aware at times that she did exist. I had been pushed off my path to emotional maturity. But the detour I took didn't send me back to the beginning. It did, however, dictate a route, involved me in drama, and slowed down my progress.

In my 40's I read <u>Unlimited Power</u> by Tony Robbins and attended his seminars in Cleveland, Detroit, California and Maui. While there

I did a 45-foot fire walk, climbed a 50-foot pole and jumped from it — all to overcome fear. I studied <u>A Course In Miracles</u> and joined a group of like-minded individuals who shared ideas and insights about the workings of the mind. I read the writings of Eckhart Tolle, Jim Parsons, Wayne Dyer, Michael Singer and others like them. I learned about Advita from those who found this Eastern spiritual philosophy so believable. So progress was made.

Through the years while on that detour, I usually heard my instincts crying out for consideration. But I was able to silence those warnings by intellectually analyzing over them or by simply following my fear.

CHAPTER 22

The final chapter of my awakening began in the late summer of 2015. I had never before experienced a full-blown panic attack. I will never forget the fear and anxiety I felt when suddenly aroused from a deep sleep in the middle of the night feeling as if I couldn't breathe. I sat up immediately, panting and gasping, feeling my heart beating like a runaway freight train. Luckily, I had enough knowledge about anxiety to understand that the best thing I could do for myself was relax. I knew I was actually breathing, or I wouldn't still be alive! Whatever caused this feeling was coming from something deep inside me. I just couldn't grab onto any thought behind the panic attack. Within a few minutes, my breathing became normal and my heart rate decreased. I laid back down in bed, wondering what had just happened and eventually went back to sleep.

These nighttime panic attacks happened three more times. Once so bad that I actually opened my front door to try and get more air. They were getting worse, and I knew I had to do something about it. I remember waking up from a dream just before the last attack. I was sitting on the sofa with my mother, my father sitting across the room. I wanted to tell her something, but I couldn't talk. Then I woke up gasping for breath. I knew this all had something to do with my being raped. But it had been almost forty years ago! How could this still be something that affected me this way.

Finally, with much trepidation, I called the Red Cross Rape Crisis Center. They had a therapist call me back to set up an appointment. I never had another panic attack after that phone call. My first appointment, I went to the wrong office and waited almost an hour before my mistake was recognized. By that time, it was too late to keep the appointment with my therapist as she had others to see. I kept telling myself this was a sign that I didn't really need to be there. I could just go home and forget about it. But I fought through those feelings and did set up another time to see this counselor. She turned out to be another gift in my life. Exactly the right person for me to talk to at exactly the right time.

She listened to everything I had to say about the home invasion rapes and assured me that facing their ramifications so many years later was totally normal. She patiently explained to me the thinking and feelings of a rapist. The operation of their brain and neediness of their own physical and psychological drives had nothing at all to do with me. I was a victim, not a participant. I could become a survivor.

What I attempted to do in 2012 was admirable. I wanted to figure out how I had involved myself in three failed marriages. I certainly dug deeply into buried truths and judgments. I faced the sad reality that my childhood had burned away most of my trust in myself, and I just didn't know how to listen to my inner instincts and choose wisely.

However, nowhere in my story about my time discovering the truths about myself and three husbands, did I mention being raped. Of course, I knew it had happened. I knew a stranger had broken into my house three times and raped me twice. It's not something one tends to forget. However, it was something I chose to ignore.

During one of my counseling sessions, I told my therapist that I never kept a diary but that I did write a lot of poetry in the 1960's, 70's and 80's. I asked if she wanted to see any of my writing. "Yes," she answered, "sometimes it allows me to see the thought processes of the person I'm working with. Then I may be able to tell where that person's thoughts and feelings were at a particular point in time." This was a new idea for me. I had never considered using my poetry as a therapy tool. So home I went to look at all those poems in a new way. I got out a copy of that book I had written for my children called Just Me and began reading through it with an eye to finding myself in my writing.

When I came to the pages of the poetry I had written around the time of my divorce from man1, I was astounded at what I saw. There was a light coming through those papers as if each page was backlit. I blinked once. Twice. The light didn't go away. In those poems, I captured the courage, the wisdom and the strength of my beginning steps into emotional maturity. As I read those poems, I realized how important they were to my recovering all my lost pieces of Self.

I always thought my awakening had begun somewhere along my path. I thought there was a time when I began to glimpse that strong, confident woman I deep down knew myself to be. I vaguely remembered a beautiful young woman making changes in her life. Going to college while working full time and raising three wonderful children. A woman with a voice to be heard and a will to be reckoned with. But where did she go? What happened to silence that voice? What killed my spirit?

Looking back, the place that she inhabited was always fuzzy, dark and unreadable. So I guess when I thought about my life, I did what anyone might do — I ignored those inner rumblings (which so needed to be heard) and just made up another story to put into its place. This wasn't a conscious alteration of the truth, for at the time I wrote it in 2012, I didn't even understand that I had come to a blank space in my story. I didn't recognize that something very important here was missing. So I put there what was closest, easiest and acceptable to both me and others. I said "I grew tired." I never felt that was quite true — and now I know IT IS NOT TRUE!

Working with my counselor I was able to recognize three other instances where I had been taken advantage of and hurt. Date rape is RAPE! I didn't even label those incidents that way. In my mind it was all my fault. I had made poor choices. I hadn't listened to my own intuition telling me to leave. I had acted as if it was all okay. I felt the mistakes were mine, the poor judgment was mine, the blame and shame and guilt were mine. Now I understand that is not true. What happened never should have happened regardless of my inability to make better choices. I was not at fault. Someone else did this to me. Carrying around all that negative energy generated by the guilt and shame of being raped was quite a burden.

Secrets don't go away just because we bury them. They simply stay beneath the surface causing rot and fear and shame deep within our psyche. Secrets make us sick. Secrets kill — if not the body at least the spirit. Without the acknowledgment, acceptance, and integration of all these difficult pieces, we can never learn the lessons from having experienced the fear, pain, hurt and sorrow that they cause. These then become the toxic residue left inside because we buried so deeply the experience itself that we never learned the lessons that it brought. I don't believe this is a voluntary process. I believe we each deal with the traumas of life as best we can. The truth works its way to the surface (conscious thinking) when we are able to deal with it. There is no judgment here — only life being life.

Now after a lot of tears and talking and learning about trauma, rape in particular, I am finally ready to add these pieces to the puzzle of my life. I am ready to include these facts as I write this newest revision to my life story. You see, it really is an awesome answer to the question that has haunted me for years — where did I go? My awakening and first steps on a path to emotional maturity were real. What stopped them? What silenced my song and stunted my growth so very many years ago? Now I know. I didn't tire of the task! I didn't give up! I didn't get dumb or go numb! I was hurt, humiliated, shamed and degraded. I was raped.

I finally understand the twists and turns my life has taken. I understand the reasons for the detours which made my journey difficult and kept me lost and lonely for so many years. I was playing the game of life without all the pieces. I was trying to make it all work without even realizing so much was missing. I reached out when I should have reached in. I gave up when I should have held out. I sang someone else's words while my own song lay silent in my soul.

Finally all the pieces have been put together — even the ugly, misshapen and difficult parts that were unearthed during those counseling sessions. I always knew someone had broken into my house in 1977 and raped me. It was a home invasion and stranger rape. Surely, to most persons hearing the story, it was an occurrence totally outside my control. Yet, I still carried guilt and shame for what had been done to me. So much so that I chose to bury the very experience itself. Can you even imagine the power of the shame I uncovered when I finally was able to look at the three times I had been date raped? How could I ever admit to anyone that those incidents occurred? And by not admitting them, especially to myself, I silently carried with me the guilt, the sinfulness, and the disgust those events provoked.

As a tear traced its way down my cheek, the counselor stopped mid-sentence and asked who the tears were for. "For me." I softly replied. "For all the times I felt the pain of guilt and shame for what someone else had done to me." That turned out to be the wall that needed to be taken down in order for true healing to begin.

Now I am ready to venture again into the challenge of living life. My long detour has ended. With all the pieces finally placed within the framework of my mind, I am able to begin again the journey to find my intuitive nature, my very soul. I would never find her on the path of that detour. That woman, as well as she tried, was still co-dependent, ashamed, guilty, afraid, intimidated and unlovable. I would need to go back to my earlier years. A time when I first felt the excitement of growth and emotional maturity. A time when I first felt free. A time when my poetry sang of hope and rebirth, of courage and strength. I needed to go back to who I was just before the humiliation and degradation of being raped. For that watershed moment sent me spinning on a detour that up until this moment kept me from becoming all I truly am.

Now, for the first time in my life, I stand face-to face with all the parts of who I am. All the goodness, all the kindness and all the hurts and scars and flaws and blemishes that make me ME. And I am proud of who I am. I am worthy of giving and receiving love. I am whole.

~

Following is the writing I did so many years ago which became that all-important key in unlocking that life-long mystery for me of where and when I'd lost my way. These poems were written just prior to, during, and soon after my divorce from man1 (mid 1970's, age 31-32.) I need to include them so I can read them again and again to remind myself that that more emotionally grownup version of me really did exist and to honor her spirit — for there were many years she simply vanished

REBIRTH
This is my beginning —
A rebirth, if you will —
An awakening to all that life really is
And can be.
What an absolutely beautiful, glorious feeling
To know that all the good and meaningful
Things in life
Are mine for the taking.
LIFE is mine.
And I thank God for showing me
The beauty of it all.
Especially the beauty of myself.

LET ME BE

Don't try to spoil it for me.
Don't try to push me back
To what I once was.
I'm different now.
I'm struggling
To hold on to what I've found.
It's worth the struggle.

ANGER

Harsh feelings
Hateful feelings
Welling up inside me
Like hot volcanic lava
Spilling over to the outside
Burning and consuming
All it touches
Leaving dusty ash
And ruin in its wake.
My anger and frustration
Touching, hurting those around me.
When anger rises,
Needs release,
Please let me be alone
To work it out, apart.
That way no one's burned
But me.

ACCEPTANCE

I can only be what I really am
No more - no less -
I don't ask that you like me,
Only that you accept my place here
As I accept yours.

I FEEL INSIDE ABOUT TO EXPLODE

THERE'S SO MUCH MORE OF ME

TO GIVE AND KNOW.

YOU AND ME

You're realistic
I'm a dreamer.
You are shallow.
I am deep.
The things you want
I have no use for.
The things I need
You cannot give.
Neither of us is right nor wrong.
We only live in different worlds.

ACCOUNTABILITY

It is so much easier
To let others manipulate me.
To let the outside
Dictate to the inside

What is to be.
But it is so unsatisfying,
So degrading,
So pitifully weak,
To allow someone else to accept the responsibility
That is truly mine.

SELF DOUBT

I am doubting my own worth.
I fight to remember
That I am strong —
An individual in my own right.
The maker of my own destiny.
I am as strong —
Or as weak —
As I allow myself to be.
I have found something
Good and lasting
Deep within me.
My hold on it is tenuous,
But it means everything to me
To hold fast to it.
I will grow stronger
Day by day,
Moment by moment,
But only if I am able
To dispel my doubts
And know that within me
Lie the answers
To my own Being.

EPILOGUE

This is the end of my story, or at least as it relates to its telling here. Really, it is never ended — not for me. My hope for you, the reader, is that in its telling I have somehow opened your mind to the importance of personal insight and shown you how incredibly enduring and persuasive can be those thoughts and ideas which fill our brains. What we tell ourselves in our minds is what we believe is true. It benefits each one of us to listen to and examine carefully how we are speaking to ourselves and whether the thoughts tumbling through our grey matter are our own or others. Do they serve our higher good? Or are they simply judgmental? Are they even true? Lessons taught us when we were very young might well have been good for us then and served the purpose of keeping us safe. However, are those very same ideas now still serving us well as adults or are they holding us back and keeping us from becoming the person we were born to be?

All thought has a genesis. Someone, somehow, somewhere, at some time planted a seed that either helped us flourish in this life or stunted our growth. Digging through the detritus of what we hold to be truth and reality can be a challenging and shattering task. But its rewards can be inconceivably wonderful and life changing. You have to pull out those weeds in order to allow your garden to thrive.

I didn't know nor recognize what held me back from ever feeling that I was really who I was meant to be. Like an ill-fitting suit, I wore a life that didn't feel quite right. That sagged where it shouldn't have and bound me in other spots. That scratched and irritated in places I never thought possible. One that pinched and hurt when I least expected it. A life so ill-suited to whom I knew myself to be, that its very discomfort drove me, in time, to seek answers. It was a long, arduous journey, and I took lots of breaks and rests while slogging through it. Of course, I wish I could have found answers sooner. But I shall never consider those long years of searching a waste of my time. For in the end I did figure out why my life wasn't working the way I wanted it to. Why, when I had followed all the rules, been a good girl, and did all that was expected of me, it still didn't work and I only ended up unhappy. Some people go to their graves never having tilled deeply the forests of their own psyche. I got the job done. It just took me a long, long time to do it. As Socrates said, "The unexamined life is not worth living."

The other factor in making this a particularly difficult undertaking for me, was the everlasting and completely unrecognized injury of having been raped. It was a trauma I buried. Something awful, ugly, and shaming that I chose not to deal with. I thought by never talking about it, never dealing with it, never even acknowledging its occurrence, it would remain hidden and my life would simply go on as if it never happened. I certainly misjudged that outcome.

Too many of us experience some difficult and life-altering trauma at some time during our lives. We've been taught to be tough and invulnerable. To not cry. To not scream. To not show anger. To not point fingers. And to forgive and forget. Forgiving is eventually where we hope to land, but I believe there are a number of steps that need to be taken before we reach that most sublime position. We must first look at that deed and the pain, both physical and emotional, which it has caused. Trauma comes in many forms. It may be bullying, physical or mental abuse, sexual assault, rape, exploitation, imposition, mistreatment, harmful, hurtful or injurious behavior. Healing won't take place until we acknowledge our wound. In so doing, it may take counseling with a professional trained especially to work in that area of expertise in which the trauma itself took place. It may mean talking with a friend, a family member, a teacher, clergy or therapist. I can guarantee you that whichever route you go, it won't be easy. It won't be pretty. It may take lots of screaming and crying, pondering and praying. But it's the work that needs to be done in order to get out the feelings that are left inside from that traumatic experience. If left hidden, unspoken, on the inside, the guilt and shame, self disgust and humiliation will rub holes in your soul that will lead to much more damage and loss than any amount of healing pursuits might cause. There is no timetable attached for any of this work. It happens as each of us is ready to deal with it. So if it took me years to find all the lost pieces of my Self, that's okay. If someone else can find the answers and put it all back together in a much shorter amount of time, that's okay, too. However we manage, however we find our healing, it's okay.

I hope by sharing my story, it becomes evident to you that no one is alone in this struggle to heal. We are, each of us, battered and scarred in some way by life's gale-force blows. Yet, if we can in our darkest moments remember we are never alone and that truth and openness are our best friends, we can find our strength to heal. We can become that authentic human being we were born to be.

I've tended my garden. I've tilled deeply its hidden ground. I've watched over, weeded and removed the pieces that no longer live to serve my purpose. My hands are rough and scratched from the sorting through and throwing out of those things that I once allowed to run rampant in my garden. And after so much time bending and bowing as I sorted through what to keep and what to purge, my back still creeks and groans at times as I stand tall and unbroken once more. But the rose I hold now in my hand is beautiful and healthy, strong and straight as it never was before. And its bloom will be perfect, as only a rose can be.

ACKNOWLEDGMENTS

With much gratitude for your love and patience to my three children, Mike, Eric, and Kathy. Thank you to my sister, Jan, for always being there for me. And to those professional healers who were there when I needed them most, Dr. Priya Ramaiah, Dr. Don Kinsley, Michelle Foraker, and Don Diamond. With humble thanks to friends and colleagues who saw so much before I ever did and to those who encouraged me to write about it. Special thanks to my wonderful daughter without whose input, love and understanding this story would never have been written.